A Setback
Is a Setup
for a Comeback

Also by Willie Jolley

It Only Takes a Minute to Change Your Life!

A
Setback
IS A
Setup
FOR A
Comeback

Willie Jolley

ST. MARTIN'S GRIFFIN ≋ NEW YORK

www.stmartins.com

Library of Congress Cataloging-in-Publication Data

Jolley, Willie.
   A setback is a setup for a comeback / Willie Jolley.
      p.   cm.
   ISBN 0-312-20349-7 (hc)
   ISBN 0-312-26773-8 (pbk)
   1. Success—Psychological aspects.   2. Problem solving.
I. Title.
   BF637.S8.J63   1999
   158.1—dc21   99-15903
                                                      CIP

First published under the title *A Setback Is a Setup for a Comeback: Turn Your Moments of Doubt and Fear into Times of Triumph*

D 14 13 12 11 10 9 8

This book is dedicated to my mother,
Catherine B. Jolley, for her years of
personal sacrifice so my brother and I
could get a quality education, and for
her constant encouragement in every
project I have ever undertaken.
God truly is a good God for blessing
us with a mother like you!
And also to my father, Levi H. Jolley,
who died so early, yet taught us so much!

Acknowledgments

◇ ◇ ◇ First, I want to thank my friend and my father, my mentor and my master, my help and my hope, my light and my Lord, my guide and my God. . . . His name is Jesus, and I am so thankful for all that He has done for me! I thank my wife Dee, who is not just my wife and the love of my life, but also my best friend, and doubles as a great copy editor and business partner. I want to thank my children, William and Sherry Latoya, for their love and support, in all my endeavors. Thanks to my brother, Noble and his family, for their great faith and support. And thanks to my in-laws, Rivers Sr., Rivers Jr., Edith and Shirley Taylor for their encouragement and support.

I am very thankful for all the people who contributed to this book. I want to thank everyone I interviewed; everyone who submitted stories; and all the people whose stories have inspired me through the years. I convey a special thanks to all my readers, Rhonda Davis Smith, David Metcalf, RaeCarol Flynn, Darlene Bryant, and Brad and Terry Thomas. And a thank you to the Chevy Chase Regional Library in Washington, D.C., for letting me "camp out" and work on this book in peace and quiet.

Thank you, thank you, thank you to everyone at St. Martin's Press. The publishers, the sales team, the publicity people, and everyone in the office, you are all wonderful—especially the person I consider the best editor in the world, Jennifer Enderlin. I must give a big thank you to my friend and super agent, Jeff Herman, for getting me to St. Martin's and for making sure that people around the globe were able to read the words and ideas of Willie Jolley. And I must give a special thanks to Rick Frishman of Planned Television Arts for telling so many people about this guy named Willie Jolley; and for introducing me to Jeff Herman. You are the best!

I thank all of my speaker friends who have been so supportive and have "schooled me" on the publishing industry— Greg Godek, Mark Victor Hanson, Jack Canfield, Harvey Mackay, Dennis Kimbro, Charlie "Tremendous" Jones, Dave and David Yoho, George Fraser, Iyanla Van Zant, and of course my buddy and mentor, Les Brown. And thank you to all my friends in the National Speakers Association, who taught me about the speaking industry and about the power of giving and sharing. Also thanks to everyone at NSA who went to bookstores and made sure my books were "face out" and kept telling people "buy that Willie Jolley book!" I could not have done it without you. You are the best friends in the world!

Finally, I thank all the radio and television stations who interviewed me and allowed me to share my messages with the world; plus all the media outlets that wrote stories and publicized my books, music, and message. And I am so grateful for all the people who have come out to see me across the country. All the people at my speeches, all the corporate groups I visited, all the students in the schools where I spoke, all my Blessed and Highly Favored Club folks, and everyone who has bought my books and tapes. I appreciate each and every one of you. And thank you to those who have stopped me in the streets, written, or E-mailed me and let me know that my words or songs made a difference. That's why I do what I do. Your encouragement was the fuel that kept the fires burning. Thank you all and may God continue to bless you and keep you. I love you madly!

In every life there comes a time

A minute when you must decide

To stand up and live your dreams

Or fall back and live your fears.

In that minute of decision,

You must grasp the vision

And seize the power

That lies deep inside of you!

Then you will see

That dreams really can and do come true

And that all things truly are possible . . .

If you can just believe!

It Only Takes a Minute . . . to Change Your Life!

It only takes a minute to learn that

A Setback is nothing but a Setup

for a Comeback!

—Willie Jolley

I have only just a minute,

Only sixty seconds in it

Forced upon me, can't refuse it,

Didn't seek it, Didn't choose it

But it's up to me to use it

I must suffer if I lose it

Give account if I abuse it

Just a tiny little minute

But an eternity is in it!

—Dr. Benjamin Mays

Contents

Foreword

The minute you make a decision and take action . . .
is the minute you change your life!

—Willie Jolley

The Starting Point

◇ ◇ ◇ It was a beautiful Saturday night in the fall of 1989. I was on my way to my nightly performance at the Newsroom Café, where I was the featured performer. I was feeling fantastic. I had just won my third WAMMIE (the Washington, D.C., version of a Grammy) for Best Jazz Singer, and I knew that both shows were sold out that night. And it turned out to be a great night with two wonderful audiences. Later that evening I was excited when I got the message that the club owner wanted to see me.

I didn't delay, because after a night like this I could see a raise and contract extension coming my way. We sat down and he said, "You were great tonight! The audiences loved you, and you've been doing really well lately. You've just won the awards for best jazz singer and best performer. You've done everything we asked, which is why this is difficult. We've decided to make a change! We like you, and we like your band, but we decided to cut costs, you know downsize, right size, human reengineer." (You can call it what you want; it still means the same thing . . . FIRED.)

"So we decided to try this new thing that's been catching on at other clubs. It's called a karaoke machine! We want to try that for about a month."

"A month?" I said. "What about my bills?" (I learned that night that nobody cares about your bills except you and the people you owe!)

I was shocked. I was hurt. I was flabbergasted. I was devastated! I couldn't believe it. I had worked so hard to build up the clientele for the club, and I was being rewarded by getting fired and replaced by a karaoke machine! I had heard about people losing their jobs, but I had never expected it to happen to me. It was a setback! A Major Setback! Yet at the same moment, it was also the start of a marvelous comeback, a comeback that has taught me that a setback really is nothing but a setup for a comeback.

The Turning Point

From that very moment I started changing my life. I went home and told my wife I was sick and tired of someone else telling me what to sing, what not to sing, when to sing, when not to sing. I was sick and tired of someone else controlling my destiny. The time had come; I was going to change my life.

I got on the phone and called my band and told them what had happened and that I had decided to go in another direction. They wished me luck, but luck was not what I was betting on; I was betting on me! I wasn't sure exactly what I was going to do, but I was sure that I was going to change my life and I knew luck was not the deciding factor . . . I was!

I had read that "the real definition of luck is when preparation meets opportunity" and that "if you don't have an opportunity then make one." I was tired of thinking like a musician, always "waiting for my break," waiting for someone to discover me and make me a star. I decided to change my thinking, change my actions, and change my results: to stop "waiting for breaks" and start "making my breaks."

I remembered a quote I'd once read about luck by Lucille Ball. She had had a setback early in her career when she had been fired by a movie studio. A studio executive fired her because he felt she was a no-talent actress. It was from that setback that she and her husband borrowed some money and created their own show. It was named *I Love Lucy,* and it became a major hit! In fact, it became the number one television show that season, and the next season, and the next season, and the next season. The *I Love Lucy* show *went on to become* one of the biggest syndicated shows ever, and Lucille Ball *went on to become* one of the greatest comedic actresses of all time. She had a famous quote about luck, which states, "I have found it to be true, that the harder I work, the luckier I get." I couldn't agree more.

I bought into this new concept of making my breaks rather than waiting for them. I started by taking a job with a junior college as a counselor. My job was to talk to students who were not doing well in school and convince them to stay in school. It was there that I started learning about the power of motivation. When the semester was over, I was offered a job with the Washington, D.C., Public Schools as a drug prevention coordinator, talking to kids about staying away from drugs and alcohol. I started speaking and found that people truly seemed to be inspired and motivated by my speeches.

After hearing me speak to kids in schools, the teachers and principals started inviting me to speak at their association meetings. From the associations meetings I got invitations to speak to other community groups. Those invitations brought forth additional invitations to speak at their churches. In the church congregations there were people who worked for major corporations who invited me to come to their companies.

From there the people at the corporations told their friends at other companies about me and things started to grow.

A short time later Les Brown, the Motivator, heard me speak and sing at a program in Washington, D.C., and asked me if I would like to be a part of a new tour he was starting with Gladys Knight called the "Motivation and Music Tour." He liked the fact that I did both motivation and music, and felt I would be a great opener for them. From there I started touring with Les and Gladys and more opportunities came. From public speaking came radio and television, then books and records. And then other tours and concerts.

Just think . . . I could still be singing in a smoky, little night-club if I hadn't been fired and replaced by a karaoke machine! In fact, sometimes I want to go back and hug that guy who fired me. He helped me learn firsthand that a setback is nothing but a setup for a comeback!

Setbacks

Have you ever had a setback? Have you ever had a problem that knocked you down? Have you ever had a situation in your life that was painful? Have you ever been disappointed? Have you ever been heartbroken? Have you ever lost something, or someone, and could not seem to get your equilibrium back? Have you ever had a dilemma where the rug was pulled out from under you and you just didn't know what to do? Well, if the answer is yes to any of these questions, this book will be of help to you.

This book is a "how-to" manual to turn your setbacks into comebacks: how to win in the face of opposition and adversity, how to turn life's lemons into lemonade, your scars into stars, and your pain into power.

Have you ever wondered why some people can make a

million dollars then lose it, make a second million, lose that, then make a third million, while others can't even make ends meet? Why is it that some people, no matter what they touch, it seems to turn to gold? Why is it? Well, they know the formula, the recipe for success, and therefore can re-create success over and over again. They have adversities, they have setbacks, but they know the formula and can consistently turn those setbacks into comebacks. This book is designed to give you the recipe for effectively turning your problems into possibilities, turning your obstacles into opportunities, and turning your setbacks into comebacks. It is also about the power of defining moments that change our lives and how we can make the most of those moments. It's not just about the power of the comeback, but also the power of the process, because there is power in the process.

In this book you will discover the excitement that is created when we turn setbacks, those moments of challenge and change, into moments of victory. You will find out how to grasp victory from the jaws of defeat and find hope in desperate situations. When you have seen that it can be done, shown how it has been done, and told "how" to do it, then you too can turn those challenging times into victorious times, turn your obstacles into opportunities, and turn your setbacks into comebacks.

The VDAD Formula

This book is divided into four parts: a four-part formula for turning any setback into a comeback. The four-point formula is called the VDAD formula and consists of (a) the Power of Vision; (b) the Power of Decision; (c) the Power of Action; and (d) the Power of Desire.

The formula is one that I have found to be consistent in turning setbacks into comebacks. Just as other formulas consistently work, so does this. If you take two parts hydrogen and mix it with one part oxygen you will get water. The same is true of this formula. When you take Vision and add Decision, add Action, and add Desire, you can, and will, turn your setbacks into comebacks.

Within the four-part VDAD formula there are twelve steps or TIPS (which stands for techniques, ideas, principles, and strategies for success). The chapters are designed to help you draw insights and ideas about how others have turned their setbacks into comebacks and how you can do the same. There are ideas, plus examples and stories, on how to turn your setbacks into comebacks. Stories of the famous and the not so famous, but stories of people who got extraordinary results by using specific tools and techniques that turned their lives around; techniques that you, too, can employ to turn your setbacks into comebacks.

The twelve steps give you a specific step-by-step, point-by-point game plan that will effectively guide you through the process of turning your setbacks into comebacks. And the twelve steps work, no matter what the setback is.

The twelve steps are:

1. **Perspective:** Check your vision. . . . What do you see? Because what you see is what you get!
2. **Recognize it's Life 101:** Sometimes you're the windshield; sometimes you're the bug!
3. **Focus on your goal:** Where are you going? If the dream is big enough, the problems don't matter!
4. **Make decisions:** You've had a setback, now you must decide what you're going to do about it!
5. **Do not panic:** There is no power in a panic! Decide to stay calm, stay collected, and stay positive!
6. **Stop and think:** Step back, look in, check out, and think up! Look at your options!

7. Take action: You can have lights, you can have cameras, but nothing happens until you take action!
8. Take responsibility: Face it, trace it, erase it, replace it!
9. Harness your anger: Use it, don't lose it!
10. Have faith: You are "Blessed and Highly Favored"!
11. Say, "Yes": Say yes to your dreams; say yes to your goals. Make a commitment to your commitment! Affirm to win, refuse to lose, and never give up!
12. Make it okay to say, It's all good. Be thankful! Have an attitude of gratitude!

At the end of each chapter I will give you some specific points that are called "Teaching Points." These are important nuggets that give us "aha's" and specific information that can make a difference in our comebacks. I have found that life often gives us "Teaching Points," but we do not see them in the midst of all the activities and information we are bombarded with. The same is true in this book. There is a lot of information, and a lot of things that can get your attention, but I do not want you to miss these specific points. They have had such a positive impact on me that I felt it was important to highlight them for you.

In writing this book I have a few specific objectives. My first objective is to inspire people, because we all need inspiration. Many people think the word *inspiration* means "that which is religious," but that is not exactly correct. Most religious information is inspirational, but inspirational information does not specifically have to be religious. Let's first define inspire.

To *inspire* means to "breathe anew." Case in point, if you heard a news report stating that John Doe expired at 10:02 A.M., you would know that the breath of life went out of him at 10:02. Well, inspire is the opposite of expire. It means that the breath of life is restored. It means to "breathe anew" into others. We have found that many people are discouraged and dejected, depressed and despondent because life has just beaten them up so much that they feel defeated. Yet when they are inspired, there is a new vitality, a new energy, that is instilled in them.

We all need inspiration at some time or other. I believe we should always look for inspiration. If we look, we will usually find it. Some find it in music or in paintings or in looking at a beautiful scene, like a sunset. Wherever we find it, we should constantly seek inspiration because in it we find renewal and refreshment.

Author and speaker Dr. Wayne Dyer says that you should try to be renewed daily, just as you cleanse and renew your outer self (your body) daily. You should also wash, feed, and renew your inner self daily. You must make inspiration a part of your daily routine; otherwise your spiritual self goes lacking and can become disjointed.

Think about what happens to most people when they wake up in the morning. They turn on the television and hear about all the murders and fires and earthquakes and tragedies and how bad the economy is (even when it is doing well, some people will be forecasting doom). And that is how they start their day. No, you need inspiration!

I know how important inspiration is to me. I make it a part of my daily routine to read and listen to positive, inspirational information. When I wake up I take time to pray and meditate and read scripture or listen to something positive because statistics show that if you read or listen to something positive in the first twenty minutes of your day your productivity will go up dramatically. Why is that?

If you woke up this morning and it was rainy and cold and wet and clammy outside, what does your body usually want to do? Go back to bed! That's right. Yet, if you wake up and the sun is shining and the birds are singing and it's a beautiful day, you are more apt to want to get up and take advantage of that day, so as not to miss one minute of it.

The same is true for your psyche. If you wake up and hear how bad things are and how many negative things happened overnight, it creates a cloud above you. You might get up but you are not enthusiastic about jumping into that day. But if you wake up and read something positive like *Lion and Gazelle,* which states:

> *Every morning in Africa a gazelle wakes up*
> *And knows that it must run faster than the fastest lion*
> *Or it will be killed and eaten.*
> *Also every morning in Africa a lion wakes up*
> *And knows that it must outrun the slowest gazelle*
> *Or it will starve to death.*
> *It doesn't matter whether you are a lion or a gazelle . . .*
> *When the sun comes up, you'd better be running!*

Or you could wake up, read some Scripture, and shout out something like this scriptural text: "This is the day, which the Lord has made, let us rejoice and be glad in it!" Or you could also simply pick up the phone and call the Willie Jolley Magnificent Motivational Minute Hotline at 1-888-2MOTIV8 (1-888-266-8488) and hear a minute of motivation taken from my book, *It Only Takes a Minute to Change Your Life!*

Whatever you do, make it a habit to wake up and start your day with that which is positive, powerful, and inspirational. When you start your day in a positive way, you begin your day with a new perspective, a new attitude, and a new excitement. You are excited about being alive; and if you are excited about being alive, you are more apt to try more. If you try more, you are more apt to achieve more. Choose to program yourself rather than letting the negative naysayers program you. Choose to win!

To inspire also means to really make a difference in the lives of others. Mother Teresa inspired millions and millions of people by giving of herself and making a difference. She said, "If I'd have never picked up the first person in Calcutta, I would have never picked up the other forty-two thousand!" Princess Diana inspired millions of people by going above and beyond the call of duty and committing herself to helping others. Mahatma Gandhi inspired millions of people because he made a commitment to help others, even if it meant personal pain and discomfort for himself. Many can "breathe anew" into others by the lives that they live and by making a commitment to make a difference.

When you are inspired, you can then share inspiration with your friends and family. For many years, when I was singing for a living, I was not interested in inspiring people, I just wanted to impress them. I would sing loud and strong and listen to the audience "ooh and ahh" and I was happy because they were impressed. But when I became a speaker, I went through some real challenging times, some difficult and painful times, that helped me to realize that I was here not just to impress but, more importantly, to inspire. Once I changed my focus and made a commitment to inspiring, not impressing, wonderful things started to happen in my life and in my career. I learned about service and sharing. Cavett Robert, the great dean of motivational speakers, said, "Service is the rent we pay for the space we occupy on earth!" Jim Rhon, the great motivational philosopher, says, "Service to many is the path that leads to greatness." Finally, Jesus Christ, the carpenter from Galilee, taught that those who are the greatest will be those who are the servants of many. Service and sharing inspiration are much more important than being served and impressing others.

Next, I want to give information. "Information is power" is how the saying goes, but it is only powerful when it is used. In order to really have power and make a difference, you must have some use, some "how to's," which are specific ways on how to use the information. If I share the information and the how to's with you, as others have shared with me, and you in turn share the information with others, who then also share it with more people, then we can create a network of people who are not afraid of setbacks. They will have a good understanding and confidence that they will grow from the setbacks and use them to propel them to future success. The key is that we must be willing to share the information (and you cannot share what you do not know, and you cannot lead where you do not go). This is why I feel it is important to share what I have learned from my failures as well as my successes, my pains as well as my joys.

When I was just starting in the music business I went to hear a great blues singer in Washington, D.C., named Mary Jefferson. She was incredible! After her performance I told her I was a jazz singer but I also wanted to learn how to sing the blues like she sang them. She smiled and said, "Baby, I can teach you the notes and the words, but that won't make you a blues singer. See baby, you've got to suffer to sing the blues!"

I have always remembered that lesson. I realized that it is nice for people to hear about my accomplishments, but it is more powerful to hear about my struggles and what I did to overcome them. We can be of service telling our successes, but we can be of greater service telling about our pains and how we made it through the storms of life.

Finally, I wanted to share my personal philosophy in this book, which includes my theological perspectives. After graduating from college I had a great "desire to inspire" and so I figured I would go to a theological seminary, since the only people I knew who dealt with inspiration were preachers. But after going for three years and getting a masters degree in theology, I realized I had not heard the call to preach. It was so bewildering. I knew I had this desire to inspire, but I had not heard the call to preach. I didn't know what to do.

It was a very painful time because no one, including myself, could understand why I had gone through all the years of college and seminary and not become a preacher. I graduated from seminary and was offered a church, but I couldn't accept it because I believed that preaching is a high calling of God and should not be entered into frivolously. If I didn't hear the call, I knew I couldn't take on that office, so I pursued my other love, entertaining.

I became a jingle singer and nightclub performer (quite a change, huh?). I sang jingles for lots of commercials and was awarded five consecutive Washington area music awards. Three for Best Male Jazz Vocalist and two for Best Inspirational Male Vocalist. I performed to standing-room-only audiences every night and had quite a bit of success. Until I had my karaoke setback, a setback that changed my life and helped me to find my destiny!

It was after that setback that I took a job with the Washington, D.C., public schools as a drug prevention coordinator and started speaking to kids abut staying away from drugs. It was during that year that I found my "speaking voice" and discovered an ability to mix motivation, inspiration, and entertainment. From there I created a concept called "InspirTainment" and took InspirTainment to kids, then to colleges and corporations, then to people across America, and then around the globe. This book will share some of my "InspirTainment philosophy," some inspiration, some motivation, some of my theological ideas, and I hope it will also be entertaining in the process.

I also want to make it clear that I will talk about my faith because I believe faith is an important ingredient in success and in overcoming challenges. I remember when my first book came out, a lawyer friend wrote, "I like your book, but I am a little confused. I thought this was a success book, and then I read about how you kept talking about God in your book. I don't understand what God has to do with success." I wrote back, "It is a success book, and therefore I have shared my philosophy on success and I believe that my faith and my success are inseparable. I cannot have one without the other. It is like trying to separate the wet from the water, the hot from the fire. My faith and my success cannot be separated!"

Throughout the book I will share tidbits and nuggets that I have found in the Bible that deal directly with success and overcoming obstacles. I truly believe that the Bible is one of the greatest success manuals ever written. It gives incredible success strategies and techniques, and a formula for success as well as a formula for turning your setbacks into powerful comebacks. Plus, according to a Gallup Poll, it is the number one most read and bestselling book of all times. According to a recent study in *USA Today,* it is a source of inspiration and information for most of today's major success stories. I have found many answers about setbacks in the Bible and it has given wonderful examples of how to turn setbacks into comebacks.

So in short, this book is about problem solving, creative thinking, motivation, leadership, and faith. If you can grasp these concepts you can turn your setbacks into comebacks. So "Tally ho, let's go" . . . It's time to turn some setbacks into comebacks!

Introduction:

It Only Takes a Minute . . . to Turn
a Setback into a Comeback!

◇ ◇ ◇ I was speaking with my friend, speaker, professor and bestselling author Dennis Kimbro, about how sad it is to see people who have had setbacks in life get knocked down and just give up. During our conversation, Dennis suggested, "Willie, we've got to help people see that a setback is not the end of the road; it's like a comeback waiting to happen!"

"You're right," I shot back. "It's like a setup for the comeback."

"Yeah!"

"Yeah! Wow, That's it, Dennis . . . a setback is really a setup for a comeback."

I believe that we must get a new way of thinking about our challenges, real and imagined. We need to view our setbacks as situations to be accepted rather than circumstances to be rejected, because if there were no setbacks, consequently there could be no comebacks. If we want to have a comeback, then we must come back from something. In other words, setbacks are prerequisites for comebacks. Adversity is also a part of the equation. Adversity and challenges are life's way of creating strength. Adversity creates challenge, and challenge creates change, and change is absolutely necessary for growth. If there is no change and challenge, there can be no growth and development.

Let's face it, most of us dread adversity and change. Someone told me that the only thing that likes change is a wet baby, but change is absolutely necessary for growth. Successful people not only embrace change but they do all they can to create it and drive it! They understand that change is a necessary part of success and in order to grow, you must be willing to change.

Are You Willing to Change?

Time changes things, so what was . . . isn't, and what is . . . soon won't be. Constant change is the only reality!

—Sid Malwhed

None of us can change our yesterdays, but ALL of us can change our tomorrows!

—Colin Powell

Do you want more in the future than you've had in the past? Do you want to be more in the future than you've been in the past? Do you want to do more in the future than you have done in the past? If the answer is yes to any of these questions, then you must change!

In order to turn setbacks into setups for comebacks, you must be willing to do some things differently and some different things. You must be willing to change! You must be willing to change your thinking, your perspective, your attitude, and your actions. And you must do it now!

I have developed a new motivational concept that effectively deals with changing your life, your attitudes, your perspectives, and your thinking. It is called "Transformation Motivation." Transformation Motivation is motivation that leads to positive action, which leads to transformation, and that transformation leads to results. Scripture says, "Be ye transformed by the renewing of your mind," which means that we are transformed by renewing and changing our thinking. Our thinking determines our actions, and our actions determine our results.

What is the key to changing your life? What is the key to turning your problems into powerful possibilities and then into realities? What is the key to turning your setbacks into comebacks? It is simple: *You must decide!* The first step in turning a setback into a comeback is that you must decide. You simply must decide to!

And how long does it take to decide and change your life? It only takes a minute! The minute you make a decision and take action, you change your life! And in order to effectively make a decision, take action, and change your life, you must have vision because your vision determines your decisions. Then your decisions determine your actions, and your actions create change.

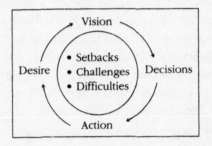

As you see, your vision determines your decision, which leads to your actions and moves to desire, which leads back to vision and the cycle begins again. In the middle of the circle there will be challenges, difficulties, and setbacks because as long as you are moving and growing through (not just going through) the success process, you will have setbacks, challenges, and difficulties. Yet these setbacks, challenges, and difficulties can be overcome by consistently employing the Vision, Decision, Action, and Desire formula, the VDAD formula. And these four components together create the mechanism for creating positive change and transformation in your life.

Vision, decision, action, and desire will transform and change your life, and they will turn your setbacks into comebacks. Now you may not reach your destination in a minute, but you certainly can change your direction in a minute! And the minute you change your direction and take action is the minute you will change your life!

Unfortunately most people want things to be different in the future but do not want to change in the present. Ramon Williamson, the success trainer, says, "Change is inevitable, but your response is optional!" Change is like a supersonic train and you have three choices. You can step in front of it and refuse to move and let it run you over. You can step back and watch it pass you by. Or you can get on board and ride it, then eventually move to the front and drive it. My mother told me as a youngster, "If you keep on doing what you've been doing, you will keep getting what you've been getting!" And it's been said, "The definition for insanity is to keep on doing the exact same thing the exact same way and expect different results!"

Change is a necessary part of life, and a necessary part of our existence. Yet change is uncomfortable. We all get used to things a certain way, and when they change we have to rearrange and readjust, and that is uncomfortable. As we go from childhood to being a teenager, we go through uncomfortable changes. As we go from being a teenager to a young adult, we go through uncomfortable changes. In each stage of life we continually go through changes, and they are uncomfortable. That is why we call them growing pains.

We might experience change in our careers by getting a new job, which means we must make new adjustments. Or we might lose a job, or have a job reversal, or get passed over on the job of our dreams. It will be uncomfortable. We might experience change in our relationships, with a breakup or divorce or the death of a loved one. We might experience a change in our personal lives, with our finances or our health or with the health of our family and friends. Change can come in a number of ways and most of them are uncomfortable, yet they happen, and we must grow from them. In fact, change is absolutely necessary for growth. And setbacks are part of the change/growth process.

Anyone who has had any measure of success has had setbacks. Be it Thomas Edison, Walt Disney, George Washington Carver, Michael Jordan, Steven Spielberg, Oprah Winfrey, or any other successful person. They have all had setbacks. The common elements are Vision (a big dream), Decision (a willingness to make tough decisions), Action (definitive action on the dream), and Desire (the commitment to keep going until you reach your goal).

One of my favorite stories is about Dr. Seuss, the children's author, who was turned down by just about every publisher in the country. Only one publisher believed in him, but that was all he needed, and he went on to have massive success. Friends, setbacks are a part of success, a major part of success; and setbacks are nothing but comebacks waiting to happen. If you have a minute, you can make a comeback.

It Only Takes a Minute!

In every comeback there is a defining minute, a defining moment that begins the transformation process and turns the tide from a negative direction to a positive direction. If you have ever noticed a sports event where one team is losing and their fate looks doomed, yet in a minute, a moment, everything changes. Momentum changes sides, energy changes sides, and the losing team starts to look and act like the winning team. It is exciting. It is captivating. It is compelling. And it enthralls the participants, as well as the observers.

We all have moments in life where we might be losing one moment but then in a flash, in only a moment everything changes. The momentum can change, the energy can change, and we change. We start anew and we learn to win. Just as in sporting events, it is exciting. It is captivating and compelling! It changes our lives as well as the lives of others. The key is to be able to create those moments and re-create them to consistently spark our comebacks. Just as some teams specialize in comebacks because they know how to comeback and turn things around, we too can specialize in comebacks and turn all of our setbacks into comebacks. Just as some teams become known as "comeback kids" because they consistently come back from impossible situations and win, we too can create the same magic. The key is to learn how to manifest the magic of that minute and turn our setbacks into comebacks.

In the final chapter of my last book, *It Only Takes a Minute to Change Your Life,* I shared some stories about people whose lives were changed in a minute. In one minute, one defining minute, these people decided to change. Most successful people can identify one minute, one moment, where their lives were changed; and it usually occurred in times of adversity. And it is in those minutes of adversity that they were able to grasp their mission and purpose.

I shared the stories of Rosa Parks, Martin Luther King Jr., Nathan Hale, and the Apostle Paul. All had incredible moments of adversity that defined them. Rosa Parks had a defining minute, a moment of major adversity, in 1955 when she refused to give up her seat on a bus and move to the back of the bus simply because of the color of her skin. She refused to move and made a decision to remain seated. She knew that she was breaking a law, but she decided that she was willing to go to jail if necessary. She was arrested and in that moment she changed her life and changed history. Martin Luther King, Jr. was a twenty-six-year-old preacher, who happened to be the new pastor of a small church in Montgomery, Alabama, at the time, who was asked to lead the bus boycott and inspire the people. He was young, new to the area, and was trying to get some stability in this new ministry, but he said, "Yes, I'll do it," and in that moment he defined his destiny and went on to change history.

Nathan Hale was captured behind the enemy line during the Revolutionary War. He was immediately sentenced to death and his handwritten note to his parents, his only communication, was torn up in front of him. Yet he made a decision to maintain his dignity and in that moment defined his destiny and changed history. As he ascended the stairs of the gallows, he stopped and said, "I only regret that I have but one life to lose for my country!" In one minute, one defining moment, he sparked a revolution. He gave a struggling band of colonists a rallying cry that inspired them and helped to forge them into an army that went on to win despite the odds.

I also shared the story of the Apostle Paul, who had a defining minute, a compelling moment, on the Damascus road that would change his life and change history. In one minute he went from being one of the greatest persecutors of this group called Christians to become the greatest defender of the faith. Defining minutes, compelling moments, that changed lives and changed history.

Oh, what a minute! Those defining moments that can make us or mold us, break us or build us, that challenge us and change us, and can possibly change history. Those moments usually are the result of adversity; they are the result of setbacks, but we must remember, if there are no setbacks there could be no comebacks. A minute can make a major difference, especially a defining minute.

What about those minutes that decimate and devastate your lives? What do you do when you are beset by problems and hit from the blind side? What do you do when you are going after your goal and life throws you a curve ball? What do you do when you get knocked to the canvas of life? What do you do when all that you have worked to create is destroyed in one quick moment? I say you must learn how to turn setbacks into comebacks. I say you must use those moments to define your future, not deflate your future. I say you must understand that a setback is nothing but a setup for a comeback.

What Is a Setback? (And What It Is Not!)

Before we get too far I believe we should make sure that we are all on the same page as to what a setback is and what it is not. We must make sure that we have a good working definition of the word *setback*. Due to varied cultural and geographic elements, we find that people may have many definitions for the same words.

I once heard Dr. Frederick K. C. Price, of Ever Increasing Faith Ministries in California, talk about the importance of semantics. He said that semantics, the common definition of words, is critical in effectively communicating ideas. Without clear, consistent definitions, there is too much room for error. Like if you were told, "I just saw a fox going down the street!" Some people would think of a little furry animal with four legs, a tail, and a pointy nose. Someone else might think of a certain brand of automobile. Then someone else might think of a very beautiful woman. It could be very confusing if you do not make it clear what kind of fox you are actually specifying. Therefore we must make sure we have a consistent and effective definition of the word *setback*.

Webster's Third New International Dictionary defines *set-

back as "a checking or progress, an unexpected reverse or defeat, a hindrance, a check, a reversal, an impediment, a block, an obstruction, a defeat, a delay, a disadvantage, a disappointment, a hold-up, a rebuff, an upset, a loss, or a relapse." Did you notice the words "Death," "the End," or "Finish" do not appear in this group? This shows that a setback is not the end! As author and consultant John Capozzi says, "A turn, or bend in the road, is not the end of the road . . . unless you fail to make the turn!"

In reality, it is not the end. It is a temporary situation that can be turned around. It is not death! Death is death, and a setback is a setback. They are not the same thing. There might be times when people have setbacks and they may appear dead. They may be on the verge of death or on the verge of giving up and calling it a done deal, but as long as there is a small spark left, there is the possibility for turning it around and coming back.

Tina Turner is a wonderful example. After years of abuse from her husband, Ike, she finally decided to leave. She disappeared from the public view and tried to get a record contract here in America but was turned down by numerous companies and told she was washed up. But Tina Turner disagreed and made up her mind that she was going to make a comeback, a big comeback! She went to Europe and recorded a song called "Let's Stay Together," which became a hit. She then came back to America and recorded an album called *What's Love Got to Do with It,* which became a massive success. She has gone on to become one of the highest grossing concert artists in the world. She proved that a setback is nothing but a setup for a comeback.

John Travolta is another example of a comeback kid in action. After a successful run on the television show *Welcome Back, Mr. Kotter,* he drifted on to do a few more shows that were not successful. Then he appeared in a few "B" movies, which were also not successful, and he just disappeared from the scene. Many thought he was done, finished, through, but he didn't. He decided to come back and started with a movie called *Pulp Fiction*. The movie was a hit, and he continued to have one hit after another. He has gone on to become one of the highest paid actors in Hollywood. A setback is nothing but a setup for a comeback.

Lee Iacocca, the automobile executive who introduced the Mustang sports car to America, was fired from Ford and left for dead. The only job he could get was with Chrysler Motors, which was on the verge of bankruptcy. Yet Iacocca turned his setback into an incredible comeback in which he not only transformed himself but he also revived and transformed Chrysler and inspired America. Lee Iacocca, John Travolta, and Tina Turner understood that like the mythical Phoenix, who rises out of the ashes, as long as there is an ember, a spark of life, you can come back!

Now let's look at the word *comeback*. Webster's Third New International Dictionary defines a *comeback* as "a return to a former position or condition; recovery, rebound, rebuttal, reply, respond, revive, retort." The key is to learn how to change your patterns and responses to consistently turn your setbacks into setups for comebacks. We must learn to see adversity as strength developers and setbacks as comeback creators.

Adversity

While prosperity best discovers vice, adversity best discovers virtue, and the virtue that comes from adversity is fortitude. The good things, which belong to prosperity, are to be wished, but the good things, which belong to adversity, are to be admired. Therefore he knows not of his own strength that has not met adversity.

—Sir Francis Bacon

If we had no winter, the spring would not be so pleasant.
If we had no adversity, then prosperity would not be so
welcome.

—Anne Bradstreet

Adversity can either break you or make you. The same
hammer that breaks the glass, also sharpens the steel.

—Bob Johnson, President of Black
Entertainment Television

Good timber does not grow with ease; the stronger the
wind, the stronger the trees.

—J. Willard Marriott

If thou faint in the time of adversity, thou strength is
small.

—Proverbs 24:10

A Perspective on Failure

You've failed many times, although you may not remember:

The first time you tried to walk, you fell down.
The first time you tried to talk, you could hardly make a
sound.
The first time you dressed yourself, you may have looked
like a clown.
But you didn't give up!
Did you hit the ball the first time you swung a bat?
Did you make a cartwheel the first time you tried that?
Did you jerk the car the first time you drove a stick?
Did you do it perfectly the first time you tried a magic trick?
Heavy hitters, the ones who hit the most home runs, also
strike out the most, when all is said and done.

Babe Ruth struck out 1,330 times, but he also hit 714 home runs.

R. H. Macy failed seven times before his store in New York caught on.

We all fail sometimes; it's a part of success. Just don't stop trying!

Don't worry about failure, Worry about the chances you miss when you don't even try . . .

Anyone who is moving ahead in life is always going to have setbacks. The only ones who don't are the people who are dead or have just given up. As long as you are alive and getting up and trying to do something with your life, you will have setbacks. Ultimately the difference between Winners and Losers and the key to long-term success is not talent or ability, chances or lucky breaks, but it is the way you view and handle setbacks and adversity. There are other things that might play a part, but the key to success will be how you handle setbacks, because sooner or later everyone has them. Losers see setbacks as the end of the road, while winners see setbacks as a bend in the road. This ultimately makes the difference between those who win and those who lose.

> *Far better to dare mighty things, to win glorious triumphs, even though checkered by failure, than to take rank with poor spirits who neither enjoy much nor suffer much, because they live in the gray twilight that knows not victory or defeat. The joy of living is his who has the heart to demand it.*
>
> —Theodore Roosevelt

In his book *Adversity Quotient,* Dr. Paul Stoltz says that there are three quotients, or standard predictors, that impact our success. There is IQ, intelligence quotient; EQ, emotional quotient; and AQ, adversity quotient. For many years most scientists and educators believed that IQ was the main predictor of success. They felt that if you had a high IQ then you were automatically destined for success. Then came Ted Kaczynski, "the Unabomber," who was a genius, but had no social skills and could not handle the pressures of life, so he became a mad bomber.

We all have seen intelligent people who have misused their intelligence and therefore never reached their potential, or who couldn't handle life's challenges and gave up; some even end up on the street begging for handouts. Intelligence alone does not guarantee success.

Daniel Goldman wrote in his book, *Emotional Intelligence,* that intelligence is not enough to guarantee success, you must have a high EQ. Goldman defines EQ as that hypothetical measurement that reflects one's ability to work and empathize with others, control impulses, make good decisions, and have high self-esteem. He states that you can be smart in more than one way. People with a high EQ tend to excel in real life with relationships, job performance, and promotions and with community activities. Goldman's findings show that many people with high IQs and low EQs fail, while their counterparts with moderate IQs and higher EQs succeed. In other words, IQ may help you get the job, but EQ will help you keep and excel in the job.

Adversity quotient on the other hand is the newest predictor of success. It states that IQ is great and EQ is wonderful, but the real determination of success is AQ, which is how you handle adversity! Dr. Stoltz says that everyone is born with a basic human drive to grow and ascend, like going up a mountain. As we go up that mountain, we will notice that achievement is not uniform; there will be fewer people (and companies) at the top rather than at the bottom. He says the reason is due to AQ, their adversity quotient.

AQ is the level of adversity that one is conditioned to go through to ascend the mountain and reach their goals. He says there are three groups and three levels of AQ. First are "the Quitters," who are the people who abandon the climb when times get tough and simply give up. The second group is called "the Campers." These are the people who start going up the mountain, get to a smooth spot, and camp out and pitch their tents there, and end up staying there. Campers tend to see change as a problem, rather than an opportunity.

The final group is called "the Climbers." Climbers are people who are committed to reaching their goals and are committed to living their dreams and being all they can be. They understand success is not a destination; it is a journey . . . a process. They might get knocked down as they move along the path, but they keep getting up and they keep going up, climbing higher and higher. Climbers are positive thinkers as well as positive doers. They keep going in spite of the obstacles. Climbers see obstacles and setbacks as a nuisance, yet as a natural part of the process. They are willing to face the problems in order to reach their goal. Campers and climbers will meet at the same place during challenging times. Campers see camp as home, while climbers see camp as a base camp, a temporary place from which to prepare to continue to climb.

Dr. Stoltz says campers who stay at the camp too long will begin to atrophy and lose their ability to climb. They get slower and weaker as time goes by. Climbers, on the other hand, get stronger and stronger as they continue to climb. They grow from their challenges and realize that adversity really does create strength. They cultivate their strength by way of their willingness to climb in the midst of adversity. Therefore climbers tend to be excellent leaders, like Mohandas Gandhi, Martin Luther King Jr., Winston Churchill, Franklin D. Roosevelt, and Nelson Mandela. Climbers are people who are willing to climb and willing to fight, despite the obstacles.

In the book *The Courage to Fail,* author Art Mortell speaks about the fact that we learn more from failure than from success. Mr. Mortell shares how all successful people realize that failure is a part of success. He writes, "Without adversity there is not growth. Adversity challenges and pushes us to accelerate the development of our greatest potential. Adversity and failure can actually become the catalyst for success." We must be willing to go through, and grow through, the challenges. We must be willing to struggle in order to really succeed!

Flight . . . Is in the Struggle!
There was a little boy walking through the forest and he came upon a cocoon of an emperor moth. He took it home so that he could watch the moth come out of the cocoon. He sat and watched for several hours as the moth struggled to force its body through the little hole. It struggled and struggled and seemed to be having a very difficult time. The little boy decided to make it easy for the butterfly, so he took out his pocketknife and cut a slit in the cocoon to allow the little butterfly to get out and help it to fly. When the butterfly appeared, it did not look like a regular butterfly. It had a swollen body and small, shriveled wings.

The little boy was upset and confused, so he ran and got his grandfather to come see the strange-looking butterfly. He told his grandfather how he had tried to make it easy for the struggling butterfly by cutting a hole in the cocoon, and how the butterfly came out and wasn't able to fly. The wise grandfather took the boy by the hand and explained that when the moth is struggling to get through the tiny hole, it is really forcing the fluid from its body into its wings. Without the struggle, the wings could not get the necessary fluid to grow. Without the struggle, the butterfly's wings would never be strong enough to function and fly, and without flight the butterfly probably would not be able to survive. Friends, the moral of the story is that flight and life are in the struggle. Without challenge and struggles we would never grow and never reach our fullest potential. Life really is in the struggle!

Frederick Douglas, the noted scholar and abolitionist of the eighteenth century, spoke passionately, throughout his life, about the need to understand the correlation between struggle and success. Frederick Douglas was an ex-slave who went on to become one of America's great statesmen by continually facing struggle after struggle and winning battle after battle because of his understanding of this paradoxical concept. Frederick Douglas wrote:

> There is no progress without struggle! Those who profess to favor freedom and yet deprecate agitation are men who want crops without plowing up the ground; they want rain without thunder and lightning. They want the ocean without the awful roar of its waters. The struggle may be a moral one or a physical one, but it must be a struggle. Men may not get all they pay for in this world, but they certainly pay for all that they get. We must do this by labor, by suffering, by sacrifice, and, if need be, by our lives.

Frederick Douglas understood that struggle is truly a major part of success.

I was out early once for my morning run and jogged by an older gentleman whom I had seen before. I said, "Good morning," and he replied the same. He asked how I was doing, and I said, "This early morning exercise is a struggle," and he replied, "Yes it is, but everything good comes with struggle!" As I ran on, I said to myself, "That is very true! Everything good that I have ever had has come with some degree of struggle. I had to struggle to get a record contract in my teens. I had to struggle through college by singing jingles and performing at nightclubs. When I started speaking, I had to struggle to start my business, then I had to struggle to build my company. I have had different types of struggle, but every achievement was the result of struggle!" Nido Qubein, the great speaker, author, and philanthropist who came to America with $50 and struggled to learn the language, and has gone on to build a multimillion-dollar empire, says "Abundance grows out of adversity and struggle."

In order to really fly, you must have some adversity. Geese fly in a "V" formation for several reasons. First, it creates a stronger team and it is easier when they all work together; there is more lift and more velocity when they work together. They also know that the harder they flap as a team, the higher they fly. They also fly in a "V" formation because it creates a system that allows everyone to face adversity and to gain strength. As the geese fly, the lead goose hits the headwinds, the most difficult position, but they do not stay there for the entire flight. As they fly, they have a rotation system. The goose in the back, which is the easiest position, gets a chance to go to the front, the hardest position. As the new goose hits the headwinds, it gets its chance to build strength. In time everyone gets a chance at the headwinds and therefore gets a chance to struggle and to grow.

The same is true for us; we need challenge in order to grow. We live in a time when people are exercising and working out like never before. Gym membership and attendance continues to increase. Those who are into weight lifting and bodybuilding know that there is a definite correlation between the size of the weight and the size and strength of the muscle; the heavier the weight, the bigger the muscle. The same is true for adversity. Little challenges create little muscles, while big challenges create big muscles. We must be willing to face adversity in order to grow. Adversity and challenges are a part of the process. And it is in times of adversity and challenge that we discover our uniqueness and experience our defining moments. Don't run from adversity and challenge. Just remember, it only takes a minute to find our greatness and it only takes a minute to turn a setback into a setup for a comeback!

Part One

The Power of Vision

Step One

Perspective: Check Your Vision. . . .
What Do You See? Because What
You See Is What You Get!

*Is there anything worse than blindness? Yes! Eyesight . . .
but no vision!*

—Helen Keller

Man is only limited by the audacity of his imagination!
—Autere

Where there is no vision, the people perish.
—Proverbs 29: 18 (KJV)

Vision

*Mediocrity is a place and it is bordered on the north by
compromise, on the south by indecision, on the east by
past thinking, and on the west by lack of vision.*
—John Mason

◇ ◇ ◇ The starting point of success, the starting point of
changing your life, and the starting point of turning your setbacks into setups for comebacks is vision. In order to turn
your setback into a setup for a comeback you must have vision! You must have a goal and you must stay focused on the

goal. Vision is the first part of the quest to turn your setback into a setup for a comeback. First, let's make sure we understand what vision is.

Vision is an image of what's possible for your life and your perspective or way of looking at life. If you have a vision of your life, then you have a view of the destination for your life and a view of what you're after. Scripture says in Proverbs 29:18 (NKJV), "Where there is no vision the people perish." What goes unsaid is, "Where there is a vision, the people will flourish!" You must have a vision in your life in order to turn your setbacks into setups for comebacks.

It is important to define the word *vision*. First, many people believe that vision means eyesight. Do you need eyesight to turn a setback into a setup for a comeback? The answer is NO! Helen Keller proved that. She was born blind and deaf, yet she became one of the greatest women of all times. Stevie Wonder proved that you do not need eyesight to become great. He was born blind and poor in Saginaw, Michigan, but he had a vision to become great and he kept trying and trying until he was discovered and signed by Motown Records. Stevie Wonder has gone on to become one of the most prolific musicians of this century. Ray Charles also had a setback as a child when he started losing his sight at the age of five. His mother didn't have the money to take him to a specialist, and he eventually went blind. He could have given up, but he decided to fight for his dream. He went on to become an American icon.

Jose Feliciano was born poor and blind in Puerto Rico. Some of the neighbors suggested that he get a cup and beg for money like blind people were supposed to do, but Jose refused! He found an "old piece of guitar" and taught himself how to play. He practiced day and night, night and day, sometimes until his fingers bled. Today Jose Feliciano is considered one of the greatest guitarists of all time. He wrote a song we sing every Christmas called *Feliz Navidad*. You don't need eyesight to turn a setback into a setup for a comeback.

The first type of vision is *eyesight*, the next type is *hindsight*, which is being able to look back at past events. Is hindsight necessary to turn a setback into a setup for a comeback? Again, no! It's good to have hindsight, so you do not repeat the mistakes of the past, but unfortunately most people who start dealing with the past get stuck in the past! They think in the past, dwell in the past, live in the past. They cannot get past the past! They dwell on what people said to them ten years ago, or what happened to them as children and then cannot get past it. I say, *The past is supposed to be a place of reference, not a place of residence! There is a reason why your car has a big windshield and a small rearview mirror. You are supposed to keep your eyes on where you are going, and just occasionally check out where you have been. . . . Otherwise you are going to crash!*

I love this quote about life. "The difference between life and school is that in school you get the lesson and then you get the test. In life you get the test and then you get the lesson." Without a test there can be no testimony. As the German philosopher Kierkegaard said, "Life is often understood backwards but must be lived forward." Learn from the past but don't dwell there.

The third type of vision is *insight!* Insight is the power to see a situation and get to the inner nature of things. It is that "still, small voice within us." Some call it *intuition*, which means "inner teacher," and others call it perspective. I see insight as being a combination of your experiences, logic, perspective, and sensitivity to your inner voice as well as to a higher voice guiding you from within. Unfortunately most people have turned the volume down. They do not listen to the voice within. They listen to all the cynics and negative people on the outside. Sometimes we need to remind ourselves of our victories and stop looking at our failures. Listen to the small voice within that says, "Look, you have had some successes and have even greater things yet to come. If you did it then, you can do it now. Just try! You can do it!" Turn up the volume on your inner voice and realize that you can do incredible things if you just try.

The last kind of sight is *foresight!* Foresight is the ability to see into the future, not as a fortune teller does, but as a person who is creating what they see in their mind. As the axiom states, "The best way to predict the future is to create it!" Foresight is about destination and determination; it is the sight that allows you to see down the road and believe what you see is possible. Scripture says, in Roman 4:17 (NKJV), that foresight is connected to faith, where you can "call forth those things that be not, as if they were." Foresight, mixed with insight, creates a powerful force called a dream; and dreams are the seeds for success. You must be willing to dream and believe that the dream is possible, no matter how many others say it is impossible. Insight and foresight mixed together are the keys to tapping into the power of vision and are the keys to starting on the comeback trail.

Perspective

Every crucial experience can be regarded either as a setback, or the start of a wonderful new adventure, it depends on your perspective!

—Mary Roberts Rinehart

We will sometimes have defeats in life but you can have defeats without being defeated, you can fail without be-

ing a failure. Winners see failure and defeats as merely
part of the process to get to win.

—Maya Angelou

Do you get upset because roses have thorns or rejoice be-
cause thorn bushes have roses?

—Author unknown

Perspective is an important part of the vision concept. Perspective means how do you view the situation? How do you
see it? Do you see this as a problem or do you see this as an
opportunity? Do you see it as a change or as a chance? Do you
see it as a new beginning or as the end? Do you see it as an
entrance or as an exit? Do you see it as the end of the road or
as a bend in the road? Do you see it as a setback "period" or
do you see it as a setback "comma"? In other words, do you
see it as the end of the sentence, or do you see it as just a
break in the sentence, a slight pause? Finally, do you see it as
a setback, or as a setup for a comeback? This is a very important question that will greatly impact how you will respond.

First, is the glass half empty or is the glass half full? Is the
night ending or is the day beginning? Whatever perspective
you choose will have a major impact on the decisions you will
make. The decisions you make will determine the actions that
you will take. Then the actions you take will determine the results you create.

Is the glass half empty or is the glass half full? This is a question I remember hearing as a child for a Peace Corps advertisement on television. At that point I wasn't exactly sure of the
answer, or the significance of the question, but it seemed to
me that there was still a lot of milk that could go in that glass.
In retrospection, I realize how fortunate I was to be brought
up by parents who were positive and who conditioned me,
from an early age, to view life from a positive perspective.

They helped me to see that the glass was half full rather than half empty. Unfortunately, far too many people are conditioned from an early age to look for, and find the glass half empty. They view life from the negative perspective. Yet even if you were conditioned that way, it doesn't mean you have to stay that way. It is a choice! I say that one of the keys to turning setbacks into comebacks is to have a positive perspective, to be able to look at the situation and decide whether it is a setback or whether it is a setup for a comeback. That is something you can choose.

Some people manage to use adversity as a motivational force, which helps to strengthen them, while others allow adversity to crush and limit them. The key is how you view adversity. You must decide to have and maintain a positive perspective. Your uplook determines your outlook, and your outlook determines your outcome, and that is when you start to realize that "yes, you know I really think I *can* make a comeback."

Wherever you find a crisis, you will also always find an opportunity. Napoleon Hill, the author of the classic book *Think and Grow Rich,* wrote: "Every adversity contains, at the same time, a seed of equivalent opportunity!" You must be willing to see that and then be willing to take the steps to turn those adverse moments into exciting, life-defining moments. The key is *how* to turn those moments of adversity around so you too can snatch victory from the jaws of defeat.

If there were no problems, there would be no opportunities! The old saying states that the key to success is to find a problem and solve it. Sometimes you don't even have to look for a problem; the problems find you. . . . You'll have a setback! When you have a setback, you also have a choice you must make. Do you see it as a setback that you should cry about or do you see it as an opportunity that you should be excited about? It truly *is* your choice. You can see it as a problem or as an opportunity. . . . It's your choice.

Doctors solve problems, and we pay them for the solution that they supply. If we have a pounding headache, we will pay to have the doctor make it go away. In fact, the worse the pain, the more we are willing to pay. The same is true for the plumber, the lawyer, the electrician, and the auto mechanic. The key is, if you want to be successful, find a need and fill it. Find a problem (or in some cases when the problem finds you), then solve it! Wherever there are problems, there are also opportunities! If there were no problems, there would be no opportunities.

Even with the challenges of life, I still say that the good greatly outweighs the bad, the happy outweighs the sad, and the pleasure outweighs the pain; but it depends on how you choose to see it. From what perspective do you choose to view it? Do you see it from a positive perspective or a negative perspective? Life is challenging, but it is also a wonderful and beautiful adventure. From the minute you are born to the minute you die you will have some beauty and you will have challenges. Anyone who doesn't is either lying or dead! You must decide what you choose to focus on. Do you look for the good or do you look for the bad?

The Power of Perspective
A large shoe company sent two sales reps out to different parts of Australia to see if they could drum up some business from the Aborigines. One rep sent a message back saying, "Waste of time, no business here. . . . Aborigines don't wear shoes." The other sent a message, "Send more troops. Great business opportunity here. Aborigines don't wear shoes!" It all depends upon how you see the glass: is it half empty or half full? That is a question that you and only you can answer. And your perspective determines your answer. Is it a positive perspective or is it a negative perspective?

Sometimes a setback will come in the form of an exit door.

You will be forced to leave something or someone and it will be uncomfortable. It might be frightening and painful because you have to leave something or someone whom you love. You will have to change, and you don't know what will result from these changes; all you know is that you have been shown the way to the door. I say you must look at this situation from a positive perspective and say, "It's okay!" That's right, say, "It's okay!" Why? *Because every exit door is also an entrance door. When you leave one place you are always entering into another place. A place filled with new possibilities and opportunities.*

You may face a future, which is unknown. I know that can be frightening, but you must have courage. Courage is not the absence of fear, but rather going forward in spite of fear. Go ahead, go forward with courage, and realize that life is a wonderful adventure. Life is a wonderful adventure for those who are willing to live it to the fullest. Just remember that every exit is also an entrance to a new place, which has new possibilities and opportunities.

The Fear of the Unknown

There was a man who was standing in front of a firing squad and was given one last wish. The captain of the guard came up and told him that he had a choice: he could face the firing squad or he could take the cave door that was way over in the dark, past the marsh and past the woods. He looked and saw a cave and asked, "Where does it lead?" The captain of the guard said, "No one knows!" He looked over again and again saw the nasty marsh and the dark woods and it looked so scary and frightening that he finally said, "Just go ahead and shoot!" And they did!

Afterward a young soldier asked if he could go and investigate the cave. The captain shuddered and said, "It's your life, but I wouldn't if I were you!" The young soldier went over toward the cave. He crawled through the swamp and trekked through the dark and came up to the cave and went in and on the other side it led to freedom, beautiful freedom. *The moral of the story is that most people would rather settle for known hells than unknown heavens.*

I remember having obstacles in the past that looked like impassable mountains, but after I had overcome them they looked more like little molehills. I believe we all experience that if we are just willing to look back and look objectively. Think back to problems in your life, or maybe just life experiences that you had to go through. Like going through high school or college. It might have seemed like a big deal before you started, but it was a lot smaller after you finished.

The Hummingbird and the Vulture!

In life you must understand that perspective is a powerful quality. If you look at the desert you will see the power of perspective. The vulture flies through the desert and focuses its energy on death. It looks for death and decay and it is not able to focus on anything else. The hummingbird also flies through the desert and it too must focus its power, but it looks for life. It looks for flowers and plants and other vegetation that it can use to sustain life. If you look for the negative, that is what you will find; but if you look for the positive, beautiful things you will find them also. In the Book of Proverbs 11:27 (RSV) it is written: "If you search for good, you will find God's favor, if you search for evil you will find His curse." *It is up to you. You can choose to look for the beauty in life or to look for the troubles in life. If you look you will find them. Decide to have a positive perspective and a positive outlook. It can change your life.*

I like this quote by Sidney J. Harris. "When I hear somebody sigh that 'life is hard,' I am always tempted to ask, 'Compared to what?' " Yes, life is challenging, but it is also filled with beautiful possibilities, it depends on your perspective. Look for the positive and realize that a setback is not the end of the road, it is just a bend in the road.

Step One: Teaching Points:

1. Without a vision a people will perish, but with a vision a people will flourish.
2. The past is supposed to be a place of reference, not a place of residence.
3. In school you get the lesson then the test, while in life you get the test then the lesson.
4. Life is to be understood backward, but must be lived forward.
5. We can have defeats without being defeated.
6. See it as a setback with a comma, rather than a setback with a period.
7. If there were no problems, there would be no opportunities.
8. Every exit is also an entrance to a new place filled with new possibilities.
9. Do not settle for known hells when you can have unknown heavens.
10. If you search for good you will find it. Therefore, decide to have a positive perspective.

Step Two

· ·

Recognize: It's Life 101 . . .
Sometimes You're the Windshield;
Sometimes You're the Bug!

These are the times that try men's souls!

—Thomas Paine

◇ ◇ ◇ Yes, these are the times that try men's souls. These are also the times that try women's souls, and children's souls, and senior citizens' souls. These are simply trying times. So were the days before you were born and so will be the days after you die. In other words, LIFE IS TRYING! Your parents had some trying times and your grandparents had some trying times and your great grandparents had trying times. And you are going to have trying times. Before we get going let's make sure this point is clear: life is challenging. It was challenging yesterday, it is challenging today, and it will be challenging tomorrow.

As a teenager I heard a song called "Desiderata" that I thought was so cool and so hip. I was sure the author had to be one of today's greatest writers. The song talked about all the things I was experiencing in life. It talked about challenge and change and how these are trying times, yet they are also wonderful times to be alive. I was excited because I felt that someone had finally described life as I saw it.

The author wrote:

Go placidly amid the noise and the haste, and remember
what peace there may be in silence. As far as possible

without surrender, be on good terms with all persons. Speak the truth quietly and clearly; and listen to others, even the dull and ignorant; they too have their story. Avoid loud and aggressive persons; they are vexations to the spirit. . . . Enjoy your achievements, as well as your plans. Keep interested in your own career, however humble; it is a real possession in the changing fortunes of time. Exercise caution in your business affairs; for the world is full of trickery. Let this not blind you to what virtue there is. . . . Take kindly the counsel of years, gracefully surrendering the things of youth. Nurture strength of spirit to shield you in sudden misfortune. But do not distress yourself with imaginings. Many fears are born of fatigue and loneliness. Beyond a wholesome discipline; be gentle with yourself. You are a child of the universe, no less than the trees and the stars; you have a right to be here. And whether or not it is clear to you, no doubt the universe is unfolding as it should. Therefore be at peace with God, and whatever your labors and aspiration, the noisy confusion of life, keep peace with your soul. With all its sham, drudgery, and broken dreams, it is still a beautiful world. Be cheerful. Strive to be happy.
Author Unknown

As I read the author's information on the back of the music I was amazed. In looking at this "hip, new piece," I found that it had been written over five hundred years ago. I finally figured out what people meant when they said, "The more things change, the more they stay the same." *Life is trying, yet it is still wonderful to be alive; that is why it is worth the effort to continue to try.*

Every day you wake up, you will be faced with trying times. Every day you wake up, you will face a new set of challenges. In M. Scott Peck's book *The Road Less Travelled,* the first line sums it up: "Life is difficult . . . period!" And it's true! Life is difficult, life is challenging, and it is hard. As long as you live, you will have some challenges and some problems. Someone once said, "In life either you have a problem, just left a problem, or you are on your way to a problem." That's life!

Let me make it clear that even though life is trying, it is also beautiful and wonderful. It offers great possibilities and wonderful challenges, which really is a good thing. Without challenges a baby would never learn to walk and thereby to run. Without challenges we would never learn to read and to hear about new ideas. Without challenges we would never grow and stretch. Without challenges we would not have the tremendous technological advances that we have come to value as a major part of our lifestyles: light bulbs, cars, planes, computers, radio, and television.

Life is about ups and downs, ins and outs, sunshine and rain. Hopefully, you will have more ups than downs, ins than outs, and more sunny days than rainy days. Without rain there would be no rainbow, and without the rain there would be no plants and food. With the challenges come strength and growth. *Life is about waves, and waves are good. If you go into a hospital and the EKG is a straight line . . . then you are dead.*

In every life there will be times of challenge and times of adversity, and I say that it is all good. Either those moments can mold you and make you or bust you and break you. Everybody, and I do mean EVERYBODY, will have problems and challenging times. It must be the rules for the game. And the rules emphatically state: "As long as you are alive, you will have some pleasure and you will have some pain, you will have some sunshine and you will have some rain, you will have ups and you will have downs, you will have smiles and sometimes you will have frowns." That's it! It's Life 101: Sometimes you're the windshield; sometimes you're the bug!

When you are the windshield, you are big and strong and invincible and have no problems. A beautiful morning, a beautiful day, a wonderful feeling and everything is going your way! You are the king or the queen of the road! Watch out, world, here you come! When you're the bug, you will keep running into obstacles. You have one challenge after another, one windshield or brick wall after another, and one problem after another. But just because you have a day when you are the bug, does not mean you have to lose! It depends on your attitude and perspective.

If you are the bug and you have a negative attitude and a negative perspective, you see the setback as THE END! You hit a windshield, an obstacle, a problem, and, WHAM, you crash, are smashed, and burn, you give up and it's over. Yet, if you have a positive attitude and a positive perspective, you see the setback as a minor daily occurrence, a part of life, a gnat in life's big ball field. When you have a positive attitude and a positive perspective, you develop something called "bounce back ability" or "resiliency." When you hit the windshield, you no longer smash and crash and die. With a positive attitude, you develop resiliency. You hit the windshield and then you bounce off, bounce up, and fly! When you bounce off the windshield, you are then thrust into a higher trajectory and you start to fly at a higher level!

Bounce back ability is a major part of turning your setbacks into setups for comebacks. Some call it bounce back ability and some call it resilience, which is the ability to recover and adjust to challenge and change. Whatever you call it, the key is that you quickly recover from the setback and refuse to let it keep you down. You don't crash, smash, burn, and die. You bounce back and bounce up and fly. To turn your setbacks into comebacks, you must have bounce back ability; therefore you must be resilient.

The Rock 'Em, Sock 'Em Bop Punching Bag

When I was a child, my brother and I would constantly have boxing matches, which sometimes ended up with us getting battered and bruised. My parents got sick of the fights and decided to channel the energy in another direction, so they bought a Rock 'em Sock 'em Bop Punching Bag. The Bop Bag was a plastic punching bag that had a weighted base and a silly face painted on the front. When inflated, you could punch the bag as much as you wanted. The trick was that due to the weighted base, the bag, and the air-filled body, the Bop Bag would always bounce back up.

My brother and I would punch on that bag for hours trying to knock it down, and it would always bounce back up. No matter how hard we hit it, the Bop Bag kept popping back up. Our friends would come over and play with it, and everyone was amazed at how it would always bounce back. After a few weeks of hitting on the bag and not being able to get it to stay down, we got tired and soon found other toys to play with. We would occasionally sneak up on it and try to knock it down; but true to form, it would always bounce back.

Life is similar. Life comes along and knocks us down and tries to keep us down, but we must be like that Rock 'em Sock 'em Bop Punching Bag and keep bouncing back up. If we do, life will eventually get tired and frustrated and leave us alone for a while and go look for someone else. Life will sneak up on us every once in a while, and give us a quick shot to see if it can keep us down, but we should be like that Bop Bag and keep bouncing back up.

Yet the question still remains: How do you bounce back? How do you become resilient? Like everything else in turning your setback into a comeback, you must decide! You must decide to have a positive attitude and decide to bounce back. I am not saying it will be easy, because it won't be. I recommend that you repeat this phrase whenever life knocks you down: "I might be down for a moment, but I am not out! I want to let the world know; I shall bounce back and I am coming back!"

The next thing to understand in Life 101 is that life happens to everyone: "Stuff" happens, "shift" happens, "change" happens. Challenging times happen to all of us! Don't take it personally because it really is not personal. Everybody gets a chance. Challenge and change is an equal opportunity employer, or destroyer, depending on how you look at it. Everybody has setbacks! I think of a sermon I heard by Rev. H. Beecher Hicks of the Metropolitan Baptist Church in Washington, D.C., called "Get Me Out Of This Mess." Reverend Hicks stated that sooner or later everyone will have a mess, which is some serious trouble in their lives, and will need to figure a way to get out of the mess. Folks, Murphy, as in Murphy's Law, happens to everyone. Everyone!

Murphy's Law!

We have all heard about Murphy's Law, which means anything that can go wrong, will go wrong, at the worst possible time. Murphy will come and visit everyone at some time or another. Murphy is the king of setbacks. He creates setbacks and makes sure that everybody has some. Some get more than their share though because they make Murphy feel at home and do not know how to make Murphy know that he is not welcome (one man recently told me that Murphy was presently living in the spare room of his house). Murphy can be counteracted; Murphy can be sent packing. How? By making it too uncomfortable for him to stay!

You can make it too uncomfortable for Murphy to stay by

making his quest to disrupt your life too hard. You make it too hard by deterring him, making him work and making him look for an easier target. It's like the people who use an antitheft device on their cars. If the thief wants the car badly enough, he or she can probably get it. The device is a deterrent; it makes it harder and makes the thief think about it twice. The thief will think about whether they really want to work so hard for your car, when there is another car up the street that doesn't have an antitheft device. You must develop a deterrent system for Murphy. The deterrent system for Murphy is called persistence, that's right . . . plain old persistence. You must just keep moving toward your goal, in spite of Murphy.

When Murphy stops by and throws you a curve ball, you must persist. You must make a determined decision that you will simply not give up. The longer you persist, the weaker Murphy will get. A great example was when I was starting on this book. I was almost through the first draft and ready to print it out and the computer crashed. Everything was gone! My book, my notes, and months of my time . . . gone. Murphy had struck! He was trying to get me to give up (because he didn't want you to read about how to get rid of him).

I started to panic, but then I stopped and reminded myself that I needed to stay calm and think. I had backed up the information on a disk, so I need not worry. I pulled out my trusty disk and put it in the A drive and hit open. Then a note came up, saying, "Disk Error, Cannot Read Disk." Oh, no! My information was gone, and the computer couldn't read the disk. I ran to another computer and tried it there, but got the same result. Then I tried my assistant's computer with the same result: "Disk Error, Cannot Read Disk."

I got in the car and took the disk to my neighborhood computer shop and asked him to help. He slipped in the disk and got the same result, but then he said, "There's a major problem with this disk; it is corrupted and the information is gone!" No!

No! No! Murphy had struck! "Okay, what are my options?" I asked. He said he didn't know, and recommended that maybe I should think about starting over again. (Obviously not the right answer!)

I went home and sat down and started to think, "What are my options? What are my options? I know I have options; I just need to think, what are my options?" I sat for a few minutes and it came to me. "Try the old disks; maybe there is something there." I ran and got my old disks and tried one. Nothing! I tried a second, nothing. I tried a third, nothing! Then I tried the last disk in my briefcase, and on the screen . . . came my book! The only thing missing was just a week's worth of information, which I still had some handwritten notes for.

I re-created that information and had my book again. Murphy had come, but he had not gotten the welcome sign: He could not stay. He had to go! In order to send Murphy away, it is crucial that you have three things: faith, focus, and follow-through. Let's start with faith.

First, you must have faith in yourself, faith in your dreams, and faith in God, who gave you the dream and gave you life and the ability to make it into a reality. You must believe that no matter what the problem, no matter what the specific challenge, you must believe that you will be all right. You must develop a faith that says that God is with you, God is for you, and that no matter how many people Murphy has in his camp, that you and God make up a majority. Therefore, you Will win!

Second, you must have focus. Focus in on what you are trying to accomplish. Go back to your goal, your mission, and your purpose. You must focus your energies, not so much on the problem, but rather on the solution. As my friend, Success Trainer Al Way says, "Success is not about hocus, pocus . . . it is about focus, focus!"

One of the traits of people who are not successful is trying to focus on too many things at the same time. Bestselling author and speaker, Zig Ziglar uses a good analogy. Zig says, if you want to start a fire on a sunny day with a magnifying glass on a pile of leaves, you must hold the magnifying glass still and focus the glass on the leaves. If you keep moving the glass, you will not have much success in starting a fire; but if you keep it still and concentrate the sun's energies, you can create a raging blaze!

Finally, you must have follow-through! Follow through on those things that you say you're going to do. You must have commitment to keep going in spite of the problem. You must keep fighting and just never give up. Murphy loves people who give up. He then settles in and decides to create constant and continuous havoc in their lives. When you resist his attempts and you persist, and keep bouncing back up and going after your goals, Murphy gets tired and goes searching for an easier target. Don't give up! Kick Murphy in the backside! Just because it is a "law" does not mean you must abide by it and let it control your life! This is one time when I will implore you to "break the law . . . break Murphy's Law!"

I remember a time I was going to speak in Connecticut. I was the keynote dinner speaker, and the client had really worked hard to make sure everything was perfect because the proceeds were going to a special youth program he had established in his parents names. I was scheduled to speak at eight o'clock P.M. so he had arranged for me to fly in by four so that I would not have to rush and would have some time before my speech. My flight was scheduled for two so I made sure to get to the airport by twelve-thirty so I wouldn't have to rush or chance missing the plane. We boarded the plane at one-thirty, and at two we started to taxi out to the runway. Everything was going great; we were right on time. Then Murphy decided to visit. The captain came on the loudspeaker and said, "Ladies and gentlemen, I hate to announce this but we have been ordered back to the terminal. There is a storm coming this way and all flights have been grounded as a precaution." AAHHHH!!! No! This can't be!

We went back to the terminal and I asked an official how long they anticipated the delay would be? The reply was, "We don't know, but we know it will be at least two hours." I decided to look at some other options. I called the train station and the trains were completely booked. I called the bus station, but the last bus of the afternoon had just left. I called about a car, but all the rental cars were booked, and the drive would put me at the speech at least two and a half hours late. So I waited for the storm to pass. The storm finally passed and then the airline made the announcement, "We have decided to cancel all remaining flights for the rest of the day. We will resume service at six A.M. tomorrow morning!" AAHHHHHHH!!! "What? Oh no, Murphy, not today; you will not win!"

At that moment I decided it was time to declare WAR on Murphy. I went to another airline and asked if they were resuming flights; they said no! I went to another airline and asked and they said no! I went to every airline, and I kept getting the same answer . . . NO! I went up to the gate of the last airline in the terminal and asked if they were flying and they said yes! They were resuming flights immediately, but they were overbooked from all the people who already had tickets from the earlier flights and they had no seats available. I said, "Can I at least exchange my ticket from Airline X for one of yours?" She said, "Yes, but I really doubt if you will get on today, but you can use it tomorrow." She gave me a little yellow coupon ticket, and I made a beeline for the gate.

I got through security and that was as far as I could get; the area was so crowded I could hardly move. I heard the boarding announcement stating that they were boarding the plane. I knew I had to get on that plane if I was going to get to that speech. I saw an airline employee and explained my situation and asked for help. She looked at my yellow coupon and said, "I think you have a chance; come with me." She took me up to the ticket agent, who said she had one seat left and was looking for a yellow coupon. I said, "That's me! I've got a yellow coupon!" I got on the plane, and about two hours later I walked into the ballroom, just as they were saying that it didn't look like I would be able to appear. I took off my coat and started speaking! I told them, "Murphy might knock you down, but he does not have to knock you out. Just keep going, keep moving, keep trying, and never give up!"

I look back at that experience and realize the power of faith, focus, and follow-through. First, it was faith that kept me going in spite of all the obstacles. I believed that somehow, someway, I was going to get to that speech. I didn't know how, but I truly believed I would get to that speech. Second, I had to remain focused on my goal. I didn't get distracted by the problems: I stayed focused on the goal and focused on finding a way to reach that goal. Finally, I followed through. I acted on my belief. Therefore, I refused to give up. I developed a speech from that experience called, "Don't Be Intimidated by the Obstacles," which states that obstacles will be all around you, but don't let them scare you. A mountain is nothing but a lot of little pieces of dirt put together. You can overcome it; just keep digging.

There is an old saying that states that sometimes you win, sometimes you lose; that's life! I choose to look at it from a different perspective, a positive perspective. *I say, sometimes you win and sometimes you learn more about how to win.* Edison said, after his thousands of failed attempts at inventing the lightbulb, that you never lose as long as you learn from your experience and grow from it. Adversity can be a great teacher!

Second, don't take it personally. Everyone has challenges and setbacks. It's like when people cut you off in traffic and you get angry and want to give them a piece of your mind. Don't do it! Don't take it personally. Let it go! Ask yourself, "Do they know me?" Or ask, "Is this going to make a difference tomorrow or in a year?" If the answer is no, then let it go! I recommend that you exercise FIDO. Use the FIDO principle, which means to Forget It and Drive On!

Forget it and drive on. Believe it or not, 99.9 percent of the time when someone cuts you off it is not personal. It can't be. They don't know you, and you don't know them. Of course you get angry. Of course you feel offended and want to get back at them, but think before you act. Do not let someone else control *how* you will act. Let them go on their way.

I love the commercial about the older gentleman who is driving his antique sports car and a young hotshot cuts him off. The older gentleman is obviously perturbed, but he remains calm and refuses to risk messing up his car, which is dear to him, to give this guy (whom he does not know) a piece of his mind. A few miles up the road he comes upon the young hotshot again, but the hotshot has hit a truck and smashed up his hot rod. The older gentleman calmly passes and smiles. Friends, use the FIDO principle: Forget It and Drive On. Don't take it personally. Focus on the goal and remember, setbacks happen to everyone!

It is important that we define the word *challenging*. Webster's says "a challenge is something that puts one's strength, will, findings, or evidence to a test." I would like to add to that definition that challenging situations are those things that put our faith, belief, and commitment to the test and in doing so help us to become stronger. Many would call challenging experiences setbacks, but Webster defines a *setback* as "a defeat." Yet at the same time it is also ". . . a checking of progress." Both these definitions are used because a setback can be a defeat, but at the same time it is a check in your progress, a check in your movement along this road of life, a necessary part of your development. Failure can be a valuable part of the formula to success.

In his book, *The Joy of Failure*, Wayne Allyn Root states:

> Failure and rejection aren't bad. They are empowering! They cannot be avoided. To accomplish anything worth accomplishing, you've got to experience some pain along the way. To succeed, to thrive, to live the life of your dreams, you must risk failure and rejection, and then keep going. You must keep moving. You must keep fighting. That's why so many individuals never get to experience the sweet smell of success, because first you must be willing to experience the joy of failure. Without pain, there is no gain. Without risk, there is no reward.

Get Back Up and Try Again!

I was reading an article in the *Washington Post* about the Thompson sextuplets, who were born in the spring of 1997, they were a blessing for the parents but created a burden and a setback to their finances and resources. The article described how the parents had not used any fertility drugs and had planned on just one child, but they had seven babies instead. One was stillborn, but the other six survived. It was a major change for the household; they only had a one-bedroom apartment and a small car, and their resources were stretched. They didn't know what to do, yet, they did not give up; they remained thankful and hopeful.

Not long after the Thompson babies were born, another family had multiple births, seven. In the media rush, the media heard about the Thompson sextuplets, picked up the story, and the American public responded in a big way. Chevrolet gave the family a van, and Fannie Mae donated a home. Howard University also donated diapers, food, and childcare, as well as the babies complete college tuition when they reached college age.

As I read the article, one line really got my attention. It spoke about how the babies were celebrating their first birthday and how one of the babies was trying to walk. She got up and then fell down and cried. Her mother ran to her, picked her up, and said, "It's alright. That is a part of growing up! You will fall down, but get back up and try again. If you don't get back up, you will never learn to walk; and if you never learn to walk, you will never learn to run! *Jessy, remember, falling down is a part of life. . . . It's okay!*"

Wow! What a message, not only for the babies, but for everybody. When we fall or get knocked down, we need to know it's okay. Get back up and keep trying. Because if you don't get back up, you will never be able to walk, and then you will never be able to run! Never give up and never stop trying. Get back up! Remember, you might be down sometimes, but you do not have to be out! It's time to comeback!

Step Two: Teaching Points:

1. Life is trying, that is why you must continue to try.
2. Life is about waves and waves are good; on an EKG a straight line means you are dead.
3. Develop resiliency so you can bounce off and fly in a higher trajectory.
4. Break the law, Murphy's Law. Keep going forward.
5. You and God make a majority.
6. Have faith, focus, follow-through.
7. Don't be intimidated by the obstacles.

8. Learn new ways to win.
9. Don't take it personally. Exercise FIDO (forget it and drive on).
10. It's okay to fall down, just get back up. Without falling and getting up, you would never learn to walk or learn to run.

Step Three

Focus on Your Goal:
Where Are You Going?
If the Dream Is Big Enough,
the Problems Don't Matter!

Nothing ever built arose to touch the skies unless someone dreamed that it should, believed that it could, and willed that it must!

—Alfred Lord Tennyson

All men dream, but not equally. Those men that dream at night in the dusty recesses of their minds, awaken to find that it was just vanity. But those that dream by day are the dangerous ones, for they dream with their eyes open, to make sure that their dreams will come true!

—T. E. Lawrence

❖ ❖ ❖ The next step in turning your setbacks into setups for comebacks is that you must focus your energies on the dream, on the vision, on your goal. You must have vision and you must have a goal, and you must realize that they are different. A goal is something you work on while a vision is something that works on you.

Sharks

In order to reach your goals and live your dreams, you must be motivated and there are two types of motivation: inspiration and desperation. Most people usually allow desperation to motivate them. They only get motivated when their backs are up against the wall and they have no other choice. Well, what would happen if they were motivated every day? The following says it best:

> Most folks don't know how fast they can swim, until there are sharks pursuing them. But the one who succeeds in life's great race is the one who wisely sets the pace. Their pace is not set as fear requires; their stroke is a result of their desire. As you're faced with the ocean of decision, are you guided by fear or by vision? Have you set your goals? Are you trying to reach high marks? Or are you still waiting to see the sharks? Is it inspiration or desperation that you need to live your dreams? It's up to you!
>
> —Author Unknown

A few years ago I had the opportunity to spend a day with multimillionaire and network marketing king, Dexter Yager. Dexter Yager is a former truck driver who built a multimillion Amway distribution network. It was one of the most intriguing days of my life. I learned a lot about success and even more about overcoming failure.

Dexter shared story after story about the power of positive thinking and the power of adversity in developing into the type of person you can be, if you are willing to dream and to fight for the dream. He also talked about setbacks and how to grow from them. During our conversation, he said something I will never forget. He said, "As you go toward your dream, you will have problems and difficulties; but if the dream is big enough . . . the problems don't matter!" I loved it! Wow! If the dream is big enough, the problems don't matter! As time went on, I read his book, *Don't Let Anybody Steal Your Dream,* and learned more about his philosophy on dreams and success. Here are some of Dexter Yager's classic quotes:

Some say, "It's hard, it's so hard! That's right it is hard! And therefore you must go at it in a hard way. You must be willing to fight for your dream and fight hard for it, and realize that as you fight you will get stronger. You might get knocked down, but keep getting up and keep fighting. Those who refuse to lose, rarely do!

The paradox of life is that success is built on inconvenience, never convenience. Those who are willing to struggle and grow from it, win. Those who are not, lose!

Struggle creates winners! Michael Jordan and George Foreman are winners who are not afraid of letting people see them struggle, in order to see them win. If you want to be a success you must not be afraid of failure and learning to grow from the failures!

Thoughts are a dime a dozen . . . but the person who puts them into practice is priceless!

Until you learn to manage your money, your time, and your thinking, you will never achieve anything of worth! Achievement is a choice!

The best way to build your future is to build yourself. The best way to build your company is to build your people!

All men are self made. Only the successful are willing to admit it!

Count your blessings rather than your problems and always fight for your dreams, and remember if the dream is big enough . . . the problems really don't matter!

If the dream is big enough, the problems don't matter. I couldn't stop thinking about that quote. All the way home, I thought about that quote and realized that it was so very true. I thought about the time my car died as I was just starting my business, but I refused to give up and things turned out great . . . when I refused to quit! If the dream is big enough and you want it badly enough, the problems don't really matter; they are simply inconveniences. Will it be easy? NO! It will be hard. It will be difficult. It will be challenging. But if the dream is big enough and you want it badly enough, it will happen.

How are you going to have a dream come true if you don't have a dream? To have a vision for your life, to know where you are going, is a critical step in turning a setback into a setup for a comeback. One thing that you must do when you have a setback is to ask yourself, "What is it that I want to achieve and where do I want to go?" If you know where you are going, you are more apt to focus your energies on reaching that destination. Imagine you are leaving for work one morning and you discover a flat tire when you go outside. Do you give up? NO! Because you know where you want to go, and you will handle this setback in order to get to that destination.

After you get the tire changed, you start out on your trip to work; but you come to a street where there is a water-main break, which has created a detour. Do you give up and go back home? No! Because you know where you want to go, so you take the detour and continue on toward your destination. You can see yourself reaching the destination and the setbacks are just that, setbacks, detours, bends in the road. If you know your destination, the setbacks are just those detours that you go over, go around, or, if necessary, go through; but you do not stop until you reach your destination.

The power of goals can be best illustrated by looking at an ant. Ants look toward the future expecting challenges, yet they remain focused on the goal and determined to reach it. If you look closely at an ant, you will see that it is an incredible creature because it never gives up. If you see an ant going along its way and you put a leaf, a stick, a brick, or anything else in its way, it will climb over it, go under it, go around it, or do whatever is necessary to get to its goal. It never stops. It will never give up. It keeps trying, keeps moving, keeps going after its goal. In fact, the only way to stop an ant and keep it from reaching its goal is to kill it! The only time an ant stops trying is when it dies!

Not only does an ant never give up, but also it is always preparing for the winter. It prepares and thinks constantly about tomorrow. The grasshopper, on the other hand, thinks only about today. The grasshopper thinks summer all summer, while the ant thinks winter all summer. When the winter comes, the ant is able to live with some comfort, while the grasshopper suffers. Our lesson is that the ant works diligently to prepare for the hard times that will come because, sooner or later, they will come.

We should all take a lesson from the ant. We should work diligently every day, and we should be committed to setting goals and going after them. We should plan for tomorrow. Giving up is not an option, no matter what obstacles are thrown in our way. No matter what problems beset us or what circumstances we find ourselves in, we must never give up.

We've got to keep going after our dreams and striving to reach our goals. We must always prepare for the future and think about the needs of winter while still in the summer. We should plan and prepare for tomorrow, today. We should put something away for a rainy day. Just as there is sunshine, there will be rain; and just as there is summer, there is going to be winter. There will be setbacks! There will be challenges! Work hard, prepare for the difficult times, and most of all . . . NEVER GIVE UP!

Ants go toward the future expecting challenges and expecting difficulties, which is why they:

1. Know what they want and know where they are going.
2. Are persistent and never give up.
3. Set goals.
4. Plan.
5. Think abut tomorrow rather than just thinking about today (grasshoppers think summer all summer, while ants think winter all summer).
6. Work hard.
7. Work smart.
8. Choose to keep going until they get what they want or die.

The ant is a wonderful example of a creature that is totally goal oriented and does not let setbacks deter it from its goal. If we can be goal oriented and stay focused on our vision for our own lives then we will start to routinely turn setbacks into setups for comebacks! Vision is the starting point for success and it is the starting point for turning a setback into a setup for a comeback. Yet, you must keep in mind that wherever there is a vision there will be setbacks. Wherever there is a vision there will be opposition, not might be, but *will be*.

Vision and Opposition: Where You Find One, You Will Always Find the Other!

Wherever you have vision, you will always have opposition. You will have some challenge to the vision. You must be aware of the opposition and make preparations for it by believing in it strongly and being willing to fight for it. When you have a BIG vision, others will find it too much and will find it uncomfortable and will try to water it down. Don't let them do it! Einstein said, "Great spirits are always faced with violent opposition from mediocre minds." You must have the vision to see, the faith to believe, the courage to do, and the strength to endure!

Rev. Willette O. Wright of the From the Heart Church Ministries in Temple Hills, Maryland, is a friend and a great preacher who shared a message in one of her sermons that hit the spot in terms of the power of a dream. She believes that in order to be successful we must take responsibility to: (a) find our dreams, (b) focus on our dreams, and (c) fight for our dreams. Find it. Focus on it. And fight for it!

First, we must find the dream, because it's hard to have a dream come true if you don't have a dream. And you must come to the realization that some of your friends will think you are crazy when you start talking about your dream and how you are going to do some incredible things in your comeback. But I implore you to dream big anyway. Every great invention, every great achievement, was the result of a big dream, and some people probably laughed at that dream, but the person did it anyway.

They All Laughed

I was a guest on the Eric St. James radio show on WOL in Washington, D.C. During the conversation I mentioned that you must have a vision if you want to change your life, but you must also realize that opposition will arrive as soon as you have a vision. Expect people to call you crazy. Expect life to throw all kinds of obstacles in the way, but do not despair. Every great person who has gone down in the annals of history has always had a vision. They have made tough decisions, taken action, and had great desire . . . and they always had opposition. Eric then mentioned a book he had read called *They All Laughed . . . from Lightbulbs to Lasers* by Ira Flatow. It is a book about people in history who did incredible things and had incredible success and how everyone laughed at them when they talked about their dreams. Every dreamer had lots of people who laughed at them, trying to discourage them.

They laughed at Thomas Edison and called him crazy when he talked about his dream of creating a bulb of light that was not a candle. They laughed at Alexander Graham Bell and called him crazy when he talked about a machine you could talk through to other people in other places. They laughed at Christopher Columbus and called him crazy when he said the world was not flat but was round. And he was willing to fall off the edge to prove it. They laughed at the Wright brothers and called them crazy when they said they would create a flying machine.

They laughed at Martin Luther King Jr. and called him crazy when he talked about having civil rights demonstrations that were nonviolent; and when he said he wanted to have a rally on the steps of the Lincoln Memorial to share his dreams with the world, they laughed. They laughed at John F. Kennedy when he said men would reach the moon before the end of the 1960s. The list goes on and on. They all laughed!

The greatest achievements were all once considered impossible. Everyone who has done incredible things always went after the impossible. They might laugh at you and your dreams, but do not despair. You will join a very prestigious club of people who know that that those who laugh last, laugh best. If you are not willing to do that which is ridiculous, you cannot achieve that which is spectacular!

Make a commitment to focus on the dream and keep it in front of you. I wrote my dream in my planner and I read it daily. Every time I open my planner, I see my dream because I have it printed on the page divider. Remember, Scripture says in Habakkuk 2:2 (RSV): "Write the vision and make it plain upon tables so that he who reads it may run the race!"

Finally, you must be willing to fight for your dream because wherever there is a vision, there will be opposition. Wherever there is a dream, there will be dream busters. And the bigger the dream, the bigger the challenges and the bigger the problems, but also the bigger the rewards! It is essential that you make a commitment to fight. You must fight back, fight forward, and fight on! You must realize that to turn a setback into a setup for a comeback, you must first find your dream, then focus on your dream, and then fight for your dream!

We can sustain and grow the dream into a massive successful venture if we are willing to fight for the dream. You must be willing to fight for the dream because life will test you! My mother used to tell me that anything worth having was worth fighting for. The same is true for your dreams. If the dream is worth having, then the dream is worth fighting for.

The bottom line is that you must have a dream and you must make it big, because the bigger the dream the bigger the rewards. As you set out to turn a setback into a comeback, remember it will not be easy. There will be problems, there will be challenges, and there will be difficulties and oppositions; but . . . if the dream is big enough, the problems don't matter! Dream Big, Fight Hard, and do not worry if people laugh because they who laugh last, laugh best!

Step Three: Teaching Points:

1. If the dream is big enough, the problems don't matter. Therefore, dream big!
2. How are you going to have a dream come true if you don't have a dream?
3. Be like an ant. Keep going until you reach your goal or die, whichever comes first.
4. Plan and prepare for tomorrow. Think summer all winter and winter all summer.
5. Know that whenever you find your vision, you will also find opposition.
6. Winners are not afraid to let people see them struggle in order to see them win.
7. Yes it's hard; therefore you must go at it in a hard way.
8. Be willing to fight for your dream.
9. If people are not laughing at your dreams, your dreams are not BIG enough.
10. Only those who are willing to try the ridiculous can achieve the spectacular.

◊ ◊ ◊ **Part Two**

The Power
of Decision

Step Four

Make Decisions: You've Had a Setback,
Now What Are You Going to Do
About It!

> *You can be the designer of your life . . . or the victim of*
> *your circumstances; it's up to you!*
>
> —Redenbach

◆ ◆ ◆ In every success manual and in every interview for this book, I found the same concept consistency. Successful people choose to be successful; they make a conscious decision to succeed. They understand that decision and choice are integral parts of the success formula. Success certainly is a choice. Why? Because successful people understand that setbacks are part of the price they must pay for success. In order to be successful, you must deal with setbacks and learn how to overcome them or they will overcome you. They understand you may not be able to control your conditions, but you can control your decisions!

You must understand the power of choice! Success is a choice! Books have stated it. Speakers have spoken about it. And life has shown it to be true. To be a success you must simply choose success, because success is not a chance; it is a choice! Rick Pitino, the coach of the Boston Celtics and the former coach of the 1996 College Champions, the Kentucky Wildcats, wrote a book called *Success Is a Choice*, which states that "success will not happen unless you choose to make it happen. Success is not a lucky break. It is not a divine right. It is not an accident of birth. Success is a choice!"

Stuff will happen that you cannot control, but ultimately success is a matter of choice. The key to turning a setback into a comeback is first to decide. In any activity in life, the first step to success is to decide. Unfortunately, most people refuse to choose and therefore choose to lose. Either you will decide for your life, or life will decide for you.

When you have a setback, there are a couple of critical choices you must make. The first choice is your perspective, how you see the setback; the second is how you respond to the setback. These are critical choices because they determine how you will proceed in dealing with the setback.

React Versus Response!

> *The circumstances that surround a man's life are not really important. It is how the man responds to the circumstances that is important. His response is the ultimate determining factor between success and failure!*
>
> —Booker T. Washington

Will you react to the problem, or will you respond to the challenge. It's up to you! Winners tend to respond, while losers tend to react! What is the difference? Well, to react means that you see the situation from a negative perspective. Let's say you took a friend to the hospital and they were given some medicine, and then later the doctor says to you, "Your friend had a reaction to the medication." Then you would know that the medicine had a negative effect on your friend. Yet if you took a friend to the hospital and they were given medicine, and later the doctor came out and said, "Your friend responded to the medication," then you would know that the medicine had a positive effect on your friend. The same is true for your life experiences. Do you react to them or do you respond to them? Are you going to react to this setback or are you going to respond to it? It's your choice.

Decision 1: You've Had a Setback; Now What Are You Going to Do About It?

Destiny is not a chance, it is a choice! It is not a thing to be waited for; it is a thing to be achieved!
—William Jennings Bryant

Your first decision when you have a setback is how are you going to view it? Is it a setback, or is it a setup for a comeback? The next decision is what are you going to do about it? Are you going to give up or are you going to keep going? Are you going to fall back or fight back? Are you going to let it stop you or let it motivate you? It is a decision that *you* must make. It is a choice that you, and only you can make. Yet the choice will have a profound impact on the results that you achieve.

Cancer? So What? It's Just a Diagnosis, Not a Death Sentence!

I was at home working on this book when I got a call from Les Brown, the great motivational speaker and author. He had just visited his doctor, who had treated him for prostate cancer, and he was not far from my house. I said, "Les, come on over." A short while later the doorbell rang and there he was. But he was not the Les Brown I was used to. He was slim and trim and looking great. I said, "Wow, you look great! Are you on a diet?" He said, "No! I'm on a live-it! I am no longer living to eat, I am eating to live, and having a ball."

Les told me he had become a vegetarian and was now

working out every day. He was excited because his doctor had just given him a clean bill of health, and he was ecstatic. We sat down and laughed and joked as usual, but then we started talking about life: life in terms of health, the challenges of life, and the faith and choices that it takes to turn those challenges around.

I told him about my new book and how I really felt it would be wonderful to have his story, in his own words, about how he had turned his cancer setback around and created a new comeback story. I said, "Les, you wrote about me in your last book, and I'd like to get the scoop about you and your comeback over cancer for my new book." Les said, "Let's do it! I want as many people as possible to hear about the fact that cancer can be beaten." He said, "I really believe God is using me to share with people the fact that while doctors give the diagnosis, God gives the prognosis. Cancer is a diagnosis, not a death sentence. It can be beaten!"

I asked Les what he had done when he was first diagnosed with cancer. Les replied, "The same thing I always do when faced with challenging situations. I went through my power steps, which are: Self-Assessment, Self-Approval, Self-Commitment, and Self-Fulfillment. I used these steps years ago when I was struggling to make a living speaking and my ex-office manager embezzled thousands of dollars from me. I used these steps when I had to sleep on the floor of my office in Detroit because I had been evicted from my apartment. I used these steps when my television show was cancelled and made history as the best-rated, fastest-cancelled television show ever, because I refused to do topics that were low down and sleazy. I used them when I had to go through the painful loss of my mother to breast cancer. I used them when my marriage to a woman I loved, Gladys Knight, broke up. And I also used the steps to overcome prostate cancer."

Once we started discussing his four steps, I was amazed that they were very similar to my VDAD steps; we just called them by different names. *Self-Assessment* is about perspective and decision. Before you act you must accept that life is difficult and challenging for everyone, especially those who are trying to achieve specific goals in their lives. Next, you make an assessment by first facing the fact that there is a problem, a challenge in your life, rather than running from it and sticking your head in the sand. Then we must assess the impact of the problem and look at it objectively. As you continue to assess the problem, you must prioritize, which means the order in which you must address the problems.

Then I asked a question that I knew the answer to but wanted to hear it anyway. "Les, why does it happen to you? What do you say about the fact that you have had all of these challenges?" Then he responded, as I knew he would. "It's like the story about the lady who had an accident and asked why had it happened to her? The ambulance driver asked her, 'Who would you suggest, Oprah?' It happens to everyone, everyone gets a turn." This confirmed my theory that some days you're the windshield, some days you're the bug. Setbacks are a part of life; they happen to everyone!

Next we discussed *Self-Approval,* which is about vision. It is about how you must see yourself and how you then determine what you need to do to overcome a challenge. First, you must feel good about yourself and believe you are capable of overcoming this issue. Second, you must focus your energies on your goal and on what you must do to achieve the goal and to remain positive in the face of the challenge. Les said that he was afraid when he got the diagnosis but realized that he had to focus on his faith rather than his fears to overcome the problem.

Next was *Self-Commitment,* which is about action. It is about having the discipline and commitment to keep trying, no matter what happens. He made some decisions that were uncomfortable yet necessary to turn the setback into a comeback. Les knew he had to lose weight, so he changed his lifestyle and made a commitment to becoming a vegetarian. He also made a commitment to exercise daily (the only other exercise he used to do was lift a pack of candy up to his mouth). He decided to work out every day, even when traveling.

Finally, Les used *Self-Fulfillment*, which is consistent with my power principle called Desire. It is to focus on how badly you want it, with a dual focus of faith and the knowledge that God is good, all the time! Even when you have challenges, trust God and have faith that He will never leave you or forsake you. And realize that to overcome your challenges you must understand the power of prayer and work on the complete person, physically, mentally, and spiritually. It takes all three parts to effectively overcome the challenges of life and find personal fulfillment. Faith, hope, and love of self and others leads to fulfillment. When you add Desire, this leads to fulfillment, which leads to empowerment; and empowerment leads to turning your obstacles into opportunities!

Les Brown shares a message of overcoming because of what he has overcome: From being born in an abandoned building and being adopted with his twin brother when he was six days old. From being labeled educably mentally retarded, flunking two grades, barely graduating high school, and never going to college to become one of the most quoted and highest paid public speakers in the world. From starting his working career as a sanitation worker to becoming a popular radio disc jockey, community activist, and then a state legislator. From cancer victim to cancer victor, Les Brown is an overcomer, who knows how to turn setbacks into setups for comebacks. As Les said in his last book, "It's Not Over Until You Win."

It truly is not over until you win! You must remember that! Never give up. Keep trying and you can turn it around! In fact, you must keep in mind that as long as you're breathing, you still have a chance, a shot, an opportunity to turn it all around! Keep living, keep trying, and never give up, and you can turn a setback into a setup for a comeback!

I Decided to Believe Mama

Another wonderful story of never giving up and staying committed to your goal is the story of Wilma Rudolph, the great track star and Olympic Medal winner. Here is a brief recap of her story and how she used vision and decision to turn her challenges into champion moments.

Wilma Rudolph was born in Clarksville, Tennessee, the seventeenth of nineteen children. Her mother was a maid and her father a store clerk. They didn't have a lot of money, but they did have a lot of love. At the age of four, little Wilma was stricken with polio and was crippled in one leg. Her parents took her to the hospital, which was about a hundred miles away, and the doctors told her family that Wilma would not walk again.

Wilma was heartbroken because she loved to run and play with her brothers and sisters. On the long ride home she kept thinking about what the doctors had said and started to cry. Her parents sat with her and told her, "Baby, I know the doctors said that you were not going to be able to run again, but I don't believe they are right. I believe God is going to heal you and that you will run again, and will run fast." Little Wilma made a decision right then and there. She said, "I heard what the doctors said, and I heard what Mama said, and I decided to believe Mama!"

She started working on herself, little by little. First, she worked on standing, then walking, then walking fast, then jogging, and then running. It was difficult, it was uncomfortable, but fifteen years later Wilma Rudolph became the first American woman to ever win three gold medals in the Olympics.

She believed that she could run. Wilma decided to do whatever was necessary to make her dream a reality. She worked on herself daily so that she could learn to run; then she took action and she did run . . . and she ran fast!

Decision and belief are keys to turning your setbacks into comebacks. You must decide and then believe in the decision. Like the story of the man who was given six months to live, but decided to live twenty-five years more. He believed he could, he believed he would, and he did! Decision and belief are powerful ingredients in turning your setbacks into comebacks.

Work on Yourself

When I first decided that I wanted to sing jingles, I called a jingle producer and asked him if I could be one of his jingle singers. He asked me if I had a jingle demonstration tape. I said no. He said if I ever got one together then I could send it in, but they had a lot of singers already and could make no guarantees I would ever get any work. I got the impression that they weren't expecting me to do the tape and follow up, which motivated me more. So I did one.

I sent the tape to the jingle producer and a few days later I called and asked what he thought. He said it needed work. I asked could he be more specific. He hesitated and said, "To be honest, you have a nice voice, but you sound too ethnic, a little too black. I need a singer who doesn't sound so ethnic." I thanked him and told him I appreciated his honesty; I would be back in touch. He said, "Okay," but I knew he figured he would never hear from me again. But he was wrong.

I started studying pop singers, and country singers and opera singers. Then I did a new demo, where I sang country, pop, and opera. He called the next day and said he was blown away. He hired me to come in and start singing jingles for him. Not long after that, he asked me to sing a jingle for a bank. I asked what style he wanted and he said pop, with a touch of country. I sang the song exactly as he described it, and he loved it. However, a few days later he called me back and said, "Willie, we need to redo the vocal." I said, "Why? I thought you loved it!" He said, "I did, but the client wanted a different sound." I said, "What kind of sound?" He then sheepishly replied, "The client wanted a black singer!" I laughed so hard I could hardly talk. I realized that due to the setback, I had created a sound where you couldn't tell what color I was. From there, I started getting calls from lots of producers. Some were for country, some were for pop, some were for opera, and some were for jazz. The key was to see every setback as an opportunity you must decide to learn from and grow from. It is a decision.

Every day I pray for wisdom and courage because I found that these two ingredients are necessary for success, personally as well as professionally. Wisdom is the ability to discern and make good decisions. Then you need courage to act on those decisions. It takes courage to take a stand on your dreams and courage to move forward to make them a reality. Wisdom to make wise decisions and courage to act on them are my constant prayer in the process of turning my setbacks into comebacks. I recommend that you pray for wisdom and courage.

Step Four: Teaching Points:

1. Remember, success is a choice, not a chance; choose to be successful.
2. Decide for life, or life will decide for you.
3. It is not the circumstances that are important, it is how you respond to the circumstances.
4. Choose to respond not react.

5. Doctors give the diagnosis; God gives the prognosis.
6. If they give you six months to live, decide to live twenty more years.
7. Remember, it's not over until you win!
8. As long as you're breathing, you've still got a chance to make a comeback.
9. Decide to work on yourself.
10. Pray for wisdom and courage every day.

Step Five

....

Do Not Panic:
There Is No Power in a Panic!
Decide to Stay Calm,
Stay Collected, and Stay Positive!

*The only "good luck" most great people ever had was be-
ing born with the ability and determination to overcome
"back luck!"*

—Channing Pollock

◆ ◆ ◆ When you have a challenge in your life, you might
not know what to do, but one thing you definitely should not
do is panic. You should not panic because there is no power
in a panic! Panic is taken from the Greek word "to choke." To
choke means to cut off, to disengage, and to disconnect. When
you panic, that is exactly what you do: You cut off the air to
your brain; and if you cut off the air to the brain, then you cannot think clearly, and if you cannot think clearly, you cannot
exercise all of your options; and if you cannot exercise your
options, you cannot make good decisions. It is clear that you
must make wise decisions if you want to turn your setbacks
into comebacks. That is why you must not panic. Panic short-
circuits the nervous system and keeps you from thinking ra-
tional thoughts. In fact, panic really makes you crazy.

History has shown multiple examples of people who panicked and lost everything. During the stock market crash of
1929, thousands of people panicked and committed suicide,

not realizing that life would go on. If you built it once, you can build it again. Do not panic, especially with extreme measures like suicide. Suicide is a permanent solution for a temporary problem, and it is usually the result of panic.

A number of years ago I was speaking at a school and a young lady waited patiently while I finished signing books and finished talking to the other students. She asked if she could talk to me in private, and I said yes. We went over to the corner of the auditorium and sat down. She told me she had just found out that she was pregnant and she didn't know what to do. She said she was afraid to tell her parents because it would break their hearts, and she thought they would hate her.

As we talked she became more and more frantic about the situation. She started crying and became hysterical and finally said that she was going to "take care of it, and herself, once and for all." I realized from her tone that she was not thinking clearly. I asked her to just take a minute and calm down so we could talk about her future in greater detail. She said she didn't think there would be a future so she could take care of it, and herself, once and for all. I looked her in the eye and asked if she was considering ending her life and the baby's life. With tears she said, "Yes!"

We sat there and talked until she calmed down, and then I told her, "I understand how you feel, and I know for sure you must not panic." She said, "How do you know? You gave a good speech but you are successful; you can't understand this." I told her that I understood it better than she could even begin to believe. See, I had also been a teenage father. I had also come from a nice family, and I too had been afraid my parents would be hurt and disappointed. At the time I did not know what to do, but I had gone and talked to my pastor and he'd told me that we all make mistakes and that God loves us and is willing to forgive us. Therefore, we should be willing to forgive ourselves. Second, the pastor told me, suicide was not a good option because it was a permanent solution for a temporary problem! Finally, he told me to go home and tell my parents. They might be disappointed, but they loved me and would not stop loving me because I had gotten a girl pregnant.

I told her my pastor had been right. I'd gone home and my parents had been disappointed, but they'd also continued to love me. They'd said that it was my responsibility and that I had to be a man and take care of my responsibilities. They'd said that even though they were disappointed, their love was unconditional. They did not love me because I did something, or stop loving me because I didn't do something else.

Her eyes grew big. "You mean *you* were a teenage father? What did you do?"

"I raised that baby and continued to get my education. I finished college and went to graduate school, while still making sure that my daughter was fed, clothed, and well educated. Today my daughter is a successful businesswoman, whom I am very proud of. I didn't panic and I didn't kill myself. Because of that I am here to talk to you today."

The young lady smiled and tears started falling from her eyes. She said she was so happy to know that things can turn out all right if you just don't give up and just don't panic. She got up and gave me a big hug and said, "Thank you, thank you, thank you." Since then she has continued to stay in touch with me. She went on to finish high school with honors and is now an honor student in college. She is on her way to success because she did not panic.

To panic is to give up rationality and take on irrationality; to give up sanity and take on insanity. Do not panic! There is absolutely no power in panic. You will need power as you turn your setbacks into setups for comebacks! Do not panic! Do not panic!

When you have a setback, make a point of staying calm, decide to stay calm. Even in moments of excitement and high anxiety, you must respond in a calm and controlled way. The more you practice staying calm, the more you will stay calm in a crisis moment. One technique is to talk to yourself and audibly say, "Stay calm; don't panic!" Then ask yourself some questions: One, will the world stop turning because of this event?" If the answer is no, then go to the second question. If the world does not stop, why should I? Talk yourself into a calm and controlled way of thinking and acting. It is crucial that you do not lose your composure because once you've lost your composure . . . you've lost the battle.

Awfulizing and Catastrophizing

Once you panic you lose your ability to think clearly; and when you lose your ability to think clearly, you make poor decisions. With poor decisions you tend to aggravate the problem or create more problems, adding loss to loss. This is called "awfulizing and catastrophizing." In other words, you create a picture of how awful things are going and then create one catastrophe after another catastrophe, all resulting from a small incident. It's like a snowball rolling down a hill, getting bigger and bigger all the time. Like a beautiful sweater that has a small thread and you pull it until the whole sweater unravels and falls completely apart.

I once heard a story about a person who had a small setback at work and lost their composure and started to panic. The person was late for work and, when reprimanded, hollered and screamed at the supervisor. The supervisor reported the behavior to the boss, and the boss asked the person if everything was alright. The person then hollered at the boss, and was subsequently sent home. The person then got into their car and sped off in a huff, failed to come to a stop at an intersection, and hit another car. When the police came, the person hollered and screamed at the police officer and was arrested for disorderly conduct. From there one problem after another occurred, all because of a small reprimand for being late. Sounds crazy? Yes, but it happens every day when people lose control of little things that then escalate into big things.

Stay Cool, Calm, and Collected! That was the catch phrase for a deodorant commercial a few years ago, yet it is a phrase that still works today, regarding how to respond to life. Think calmly, speak calmly, and act calmly. It may not be easy but it is still a choice, a decision. You can either fly off the handle, fall apart, and go crazy; or you can choose to stay calm and collected. Choose to stay calm and collected. Realize that no matter how bad today is, tomorrow is coming!

Author and speaker, Dr. Anthony Campola, who is considered one of America's great theologians, has a wonderful speech called "It's Friday but Sunday's a-Coming" that speaks to the fact that we, like Christ, will have some Friday situations in our lives. When we have Friday situations, we will be faced with impossible odds; but we should not panic because Sunday is on the way, and Sunday brings certain victory. Sunday brings a brand-new day and a brand-new opportunity where you can and will win. We all occasionally have Friday situations in our lives, but be confident that Sunday is on the way.

In the Broadway play *Annie* there is a wonderful song titled "Tomorrow" that speaks to the fact that no matter what problems you might have today, no matter what challenges you might have today, have hope and remember that the sun "will" come out tomorrow. Have faith and believe that tomorrow brings a brand-new day, a brand-new opportunity to turn those problems around and to turn those setbacks into comebacks. You will have setbacks but as Scripture says, "it came to pass"; therefore it did not come to stay. You might have some Friday situations, some major setbacks, but always remember that Sunday, the sure victory, is on the way. Just don't panic, 'cause Sunday is a-coming, and the sun will come out tomorrow—just keep going!

Maintain a Positive Attitude!

Gravity is a fact, but airplanes circumvent that fact on an hourly basis.

—Neil Armstrong

Your attitude is more important than the facts!

—Ken Meninger

The fact is that Muggsy Bogues was born short of stature, but his attitude was that he wanted to play professional basketball, and he did it. Roger Crawford, the bestselling author and speaker, and semipro tennis player, was born without hands and with only one leg, but his attitude is "that is only an inconvenience." He says that he cannot eat with chopsticks or play chopsticks on the piano, but he has gone on to become a national tennis champion, as well as a world-renowned speaker and author of the national bestseller, *How High Can You Bounce?* He exemplifies the statement that it is your attitude, not your aptitude, that ultimately determines your altitude.

Attitude is a choice. It is a decision. Decide to have a positive attitude! As motivational speaker Dennis S. Brown says, "The only difference between a good day and a bad day is your attitude." You must choose it. We can all have short-term happiness, even if we have a bad attitude. We might buy a car or get a job or meet someone who is Mr. or Ms. "Right" and we will be happy . . . for the moment. In order to maintain that happiness and sustain that happiness, you must develop a positive attitude, because the car will get older and will eventually need servicing, the job could change and change fast, and Mr. or Ms. "Right" could become Mr. or Ms. "Wrong!" In order to overcome the challenges and problems of life it is essential that you have a positive attitude, mentally and emotionally. You need a positive mental attitude so you can think in a positive manner and a positive emotional attitude so you can act in a positive way.

A great example of changing your attitude for success is demonstrated by Joe Louis Dudley Sr. Joe Louis Dudley Sr. is the president of Dudley Products, Inc., and a great American. His is a tremendous story of how personal struggle and a positive attitude were the keys to turning his setback into an incredible comeback.

When I interviewed Joe Dudley he started out by saying, "This is hard for me, because for me to put my story in detail is like trying to put a watermelon in a soda bottle." He was right! Joe Dudley was born on a farm in Aurora, North Carolina, the fifth of eleven children. As a child he was labeled "a slow learner," retained in the first grade, and laughed at because he had a severe speech impediment. But his mother always told him to believe in himself and that he could do incredible things if he just decided to. Through his early years he never decided to. He bought into the "slow" label and acted like he was slow.

Throughout his school years Joe Dudley had a bad attitude. He became a problem child, always getting in trouble and misbehaving. Finally, in high school he met a girl who changed his life. She was the prettiest girl in the town, and he fell in love with her. He changed his attitude and was planning to marry her. One day she called him and told him she was leaving him for another guy. When he asked her why, she said, "Because he is smart and you are dumb!" It broke his heart, and all the people in the town laughed at him. He started moving back toward his old attitude, but he realized that he had to make a choice and he decided he needed to change, and change for good. He decided to maintain a positive attitude and prove to everyone that he was a smart guy.

Joe decided to become the person his mother had always said he could be. He remembered how she had always told him to "fool 'em, Joe, fool 'em!" He decided to "fool 'em" and make himself "smart." He decided to work on himself. He went back and got his first-grade books and read them. Then he got his second-grade books and read them. Then his third, fourth, fifth, all the way up to his twelfth-grade books. He said, "I might be slow, but I'm sure that when a slow one's got it . . . he's truly got it!"

He went on to North Carolina A&T and while there he invested ten dollars in a Fuller Brush Company products sales kit. He sold Fuller products door to door to support himself in college. During college he met another lady, who was more beautiful than the first girl. They got married, but now he had a new attitude and a new belief in himself. He continued to sell door to door even after graduation. He moved to New York and soon built the highest grossing Fuller branch in America. When Fuller products could not keep up with his customer demands, he started developing his own products to make sure that his customers were satisfied. In 1975, he launched Dudley Products, Inc., with his wife and three children making hair care and cosmetics products in the kitchen.

Since then he has gone on to build a multimillion-dollar organization that includes a massive cosmetology university, nineteen beauty schools, and a number of offices strategically placed around the world. He has written a bestselling book titled *Walking by Faith: I Am, I Can, and I Will*. In 1995, he was awarded the prestigious Horatio Alger Award of Excellence, given to people who have made remarkable comebacks. He has proven that your past does not equal your future and that someone else's definition and diagnosis of you does not have to be your definition and diagnosis. Finally, Joe Dudley has proven that if you decide you can win with whatever hand you are given, you will win. It just depends on your attitude. He proved that even a slow one . . . when he's got it, he's truly got it!

With a positive attitude you can find some good in the bad and some happiness in the sad. With a positive attitude you expect good things to come your way, and you therefore attract good things your way. With a positive attitude you tend to be more enthusiastic about life, and therefore life will be more enthusiastic about you. With a positive attitude you simply handle problems better!

It's all about attitude. You must have a positive attitude. And how do you get a positive attitude? You decide to. It is a decision. It is a choice. You cannot control what happens to you. You cannot control what happens around you, but you can control what happens in you. Choose to have a positive attitude.

Keep my words positive, because my words become behaviors.
Keep my behaviors positive, because my behaviors become habits.
Keep my habits positive, because my habits become my values.
Keep my values positive, because they become my destiny.

—Mahatma Gandhi

Because I'm Special
Because I'm Special, I have my sense of self
And it's not for sale, I know who I am
And I refuse to fail, I know who I am
I've got the power to succeed, And in the spirit of faith
I've got all that I need
A blessing in disguise, as evidence of things not seen,

Is the secret of success, in the seed of self-esteem,
Because I am, that I am, there's no way I can let myself down,
Hang-ups and setbacks are only stepping stones to higher ground,
Because I am Special, I am who I am

—Danny Queen

Your Input Determines Your Output!

"You are what you eat." That is what all the diet books say about your health. And computer people talk about GIGO, which means, "garbage in, garbage out!" The same is true for life. You are what you put in. Author Dennis Waitley talks about the fact that if you take an orange and squeeze it, what will come out? Orange juice! If you squeeze a grape, what will come out? Grape juice! Why? Because when pressure is applied, the true internal essence will come out. Whatever you put into your mind is essentially what you will become. That is why you must make a commitment to putting in positive information, on a daily basis. Life throws challenges at us regularly and can apply extreme pressure. Life can become overwhelming, especially if you don't have a base from which to offset the challenges. It is critical that you use great care in what goes in your mind and in your spirit. You must be careful to not allow your mind and spirit to be infected by negative influences. It all adds up to attitude. Decide to have a positive attitude.

Attitude Is Everything!
Don't Tighten up . . . Lighten up!

Keith Harrell is a friend who was one of the contributing writers, along with myself and a group of speakers, in a book called *Only the Best on Success!* Keith has a great story about overcoming setbacks and turning them into comebacks. Keith worked for IBM for fourteen years and expected to be there until he retired. Yet one Friday afternoon, Keith and 650 of his coworkers were asked to come to a special meeting. At the meeting they were told that IBM was announcing their first layoff in their sixty-five-year history. They were told that 80 percent of those employees would be gone in three months.

Keith shared with me that at that moment fear was in the room, uncertainty was in the room, anxiety was gripping the crowd, some were shaking and getting physically ill. After the announcement was made, Keith jumped up and said, "I have a question!" He was asked, "What is your question, young man?" Keith replied, "Well, sir, once the eighty percent are gone . . . can I get a bigger office, one with a window view?" The room broke up in laughter. Keith said he realized that humor was necessary at that moment to help people to get a grip and to keep them from falling apart. A good friend nudged him and said, "Hey, Keith . . . Mr. Positive, you know you'll probably be the first to go!" And HE WAS!!!!! He was fired from a job that he'd thought he would have for life, a job he was planning to retire from. He had a major setback!

Keith didn't fall apart. He had been reading the positive books and listening to the motivational tapes, and he had developed a positive attitude. Keith took that positive attitude and mixed that with a positive aptitude. He started working on his dream of being a speaker and trainer and decided to share with others how to handle change with a positive attitude. He went on to build a multimillion-dollar motivational speaking and training company. He is the author of the book *Attitude Is Everything: A Tuneup to Enhance Your Life* and is well known in boardrooms across the country as "Mr. Superfantastic" because of his greeting to all of his audiences, where he says, "When people ask you how you are doing, just say . . . Superfantastic!"

Be Optimistic . . . You Just Might End Up as President
I was in my office late one night and decided to take a break.

I flipped on the television to catch the news, and as I flipped the channels I came upon a special about Ronald Reagan. It caught my attention and I became captivated by his story. Whether you like Ronald Reagan or not, I think you can get a gem from his story.

We all know Ronald Reagan was a former B-movie actor who went on to become the president of the United States, but there was a lot more to his story. Ronald Reagan grew up in Dixon, Illinois, where he played sports through high school, was in the drama club, and served as president of the student council. He then went on to Eureka College, where he played football, was active in drama, and became president of the student body.

After college he went back to Dixon to find a job. He had his eye on a position at the new Montgomery Ward store in town. He was excited about the job and was looking forward to the money he would make, but . . . he had a setback! He was passed over and didn't get the job. He was disappointed, but he remembered his mother had told him to always remain optimistic and expect good things to result from his actions. He decided to try another direction and took a job at a small radio station. That job led to a position at a larger radio station, where he broadcast football and other sports events. In 1937, he traveled to California to report on spring training for the Chicago Cubs and got a friend to get him a screen test for Warner Brothers Studios. The studio loved him and he signed a contract.

Reagan went on to become a star and appeared in over fifty films. Then he had another setback. After the war, the movie business changed, and he was not in demand anymore. He was no longer getting work and was struggling to pay his bills, so he took a job on television hosting *The General Electric Theater*. Television was still young and many respectable actors saw it as a step down, a setback, but Ronald Reagan was optimistic and saw it as a setup for a comeback.

It was during this time as the spokesman for General Electric that he was asked to go around the country and give public relations speeches to chambers of commerce and civic groups. During the tour he was able to prime his speaking style and find what issues America's workers were concerned about on a firsthand basis.

From there, he started developing his own political position, and in 1966, he ran for governor of California. Many considered it a joke that this former actor and commercial pitchman would run for governor, and against a popular incumbent at that! They laughed, but Ronald Reagan remained optimistic . . . and WON, in a landslide election.

After two terms as governor, he decided to run for president, but did not win the nomination. He remained optimistic and ran again four years later, but lost a second time. Still he remained optimistic and decided to try again four years later, and this time he won and went on to win the national election in a landslide victory. He had had setbacks, but he had been optimistic and realized that a setback was nothing but a setup for a comeback. In his presidency his trademark was his confidence and unbridled optimism, and he continued to show us that a setback is really nothing but a setup for a comeback. History will remember him as an actor who went on to become a president because he was always optimistic, confident, and positive and realized that a setback was nothing but a setup for a comeback.

One of the most important factors affecting your attitude is the people you associate with. You must make a clear decision to stop hanging around with negative, small-minded people. They will poison your possibility thinking and therefore hinder your turning your setback into a setup for a comeback.

People with Possibility Blindness

One of the keys to overcoming setbacks is to stay away from negative people who will try to talk you out of getting up and living your dreams. You must also align yourself with positive people who will encourage you. Many times when you have setbacks you will have friends and family members who will try to talk you out of trying again. They will say, "Don't try to do that! You know you just had a setback and it will be painful if you don't make it!" Or they will say, "Aunt Susie tried to do that and she didn't make it. Don't try. It will be painful if you don't make it!" Friends, I have found that the majority of people who try to talk you out of going after your dream are not trying to be mean spirited; they just happen to suffer from possibility blindness! Since it didn't happen for them or for someone else, then they think it cannot happen for you! WRONG! That is not true! Nothing is more rewarding than to watch someone who says it can't be done get interrupted by someone who is actually doing it!

To tell people you love, to stop trying when they fall down is the same as telling the baby, "Don't try to walk anymore. You fell down so just stay down. It will be painful!" Of course it will be painful; but without falling down, the baby will never learn to walk. If you are not willing to fail, it is really difficult to be able to succeed.

Michael Jordan, who is said to be the greatest basketball player of all times, spoke on a television commercial about his failures and how they were the reason for his success. He said, "I have missed more than nine thousand shots in my career. I have lost almost three hundred games. On twenty-six occasions I have been entrusted to take the game's winning shot . . . and missed. And I have failed over and over and over again in my life. And that is why . . . I succeed." It is because of his willingness to fail, his willingness to take risks, that he is able to succeed.

Decide to be more excited about winning than afraid of losing. It's a choice. Decide to get and keep a positive attitude; it's a choice. Remember that people with a positive attitude attract more good to themselves than people with negative attitudes. So choose not to worry. Choose to be positive and choose to stay calm and collected and connected. As Bobby McFerrin sang, "Don't Worry, Be Happy!" How? Choose to. It is a choice!

The following verse was submitted by Janice Krouskop:

> ### *Why Worry?*
> *There are only two things to worry about;*
> *Either you are well or you are sick.*
> *If you are well, there is nothing to worry about.*
> *If you are sick, there are two things to worry about;*
> *Either you will get well or you will die.*
> *If you get well, there is nothing to worry about.*
> *If you die, there are only two things to worry about;*
> *Either you will go to Heaven or you will go to Hell.*
> *If you go to Heaven, there is nothing to worry about.*
> *If you go to Hell, well . . . why worry now! It's Too Late!*
> —Author Unknown

Step Five: Teaching Points:

1. Do not panic. There's no power in a panic.
2. Practice and talk yourself into being calm.
3. Do not awfulize and catastrophize; stop adding loss to loss.
4. When you have "Friday" situations, remember that "Sunday" is on the way.
5. No matter how bad things are today, tomorrow is on the way. The sun will come out tomorrow. Hold on!

6. Remember, your attitude is more important than the facts.
7. Decide to win with whatever hand you're given.
8. Don't tighten up, lighten up.
9. Nothing is more rewarding than to watch those who say it can't be done get interrupted by those actually doing it.
10. Take a chance and be willing to fail, because only then can you truly succeed.

Step Six

Stop and Think:
Step Back, Look In,
Check Out, and Think Up!
Look at Your Options!

To attract and magnetize your dreams, you must mentally reduce all obstacles to be smaller than an air particle, so in your mind they don't exist. This way it is with exhilaration that you will take the required action to accomplish your joyful goals.

—Daniel Jingwa, Author of *Blue Sky Thinking*

◇ ◇ ◇ The next step to turning a setback into a setup for a comeback is to think up new ideas. Be resourceful and check out all of your options. In order to turn a setback into a setup for a comeback, you must step back, look in, check out, and think up. You must be able to think about possibilities. If there are truly no options, then you must think about ways to create some. In other words, you must be resourceful.

Stop and Think!

Once you have made the decision to remain calm in the midst of the storm, and you have decided not to panic, you must decide to remain positive. You must start thinking about your options. At some point you need to simply stop running and start thinking; even if it is only for a short time, even just for a minute. When you stop and think, you can usually come up with some new, creative ways to reach your goals.

In order to stop and think, I recommend these four steps: (a) step back, (b) check out, (c) look in, (d) think up!

Step Back!

When challenging times occur, we need to make a conscious decision to step back from the situation and become an observer, and look objectively at the problem. Before you can effectively fix a problem, you must know what you're facing. Stop, step back, and give yourself some space. Put some distance between you and the problem.

Check Out!

Once you step back and give yourself some space, then you need to check out the problem, "size up" the situation, and objectively look at the problem. After you "size it up," then you need to "size it down," which means to mentally limit the scope and breadth of the problem.

Typically in the anxiety of the moment things tend to look bigger and tend to get blown out of proportion. Many times people look at situations to size them up, and in their minds they make the problem much bigger than it really is, which discourages them from trying. When you "size it down," you bring it down to size and make it smaller and less imposing.

Case in point, I spoke earlier of the time when I was almost finished with this book and my computer crashed and I lost a week's worth of data. It was a setback, but I had a choice of how I could face it. I could either say, "I lost all of my work from a whole week" or "I only lost a week's worth." Which do you think is easier to recover from? The second one, of course! I faced it, sized it up, then sized it down with, "It was only a week's worth; I can handle that!" Use words that keep you from blowing the problem out of proportion and keep it manageable in your mind. Once you have checked out the problem and sized it down, you can then start to solve it, piece by piece. Size it down and realize it is a molehill, not a mountain.

Look In

Next, you need to have an inward prospective to tap into your wealth of information and experience, your inner genius. If you are over ten years old then you have a wealth of information in your mental computer. To be alive and to be of an age where you have some self-sufficiency and your parents don't have to feed and dress you, then you have already overcome many problems. We have all had challenges and difficulties that we have overcome; now you must remember those times. First, you must remind yourself of your past accomplishments; and second, you must remember what you did. We can learn from the past, but we must not dwell on the past. Look back and ask yourself, "What did I do to overcome those problems in the past?" Once you come up with the answers, you can implement some of those strategies and start to work on your future responses. You have a lot of information and ideas within you, but you must look within to grasp your genius.

Think Up!

You have stopped, stepped back, and gotten some space, and you have checked it out and looked at the problem and effectively sized it down. You have gone back to your vast experience bank and thought back on strategies that have helped you in the past. Now, it is time to "think up" and look at your options. As we said earlier, you always have options, even when it seems as though you have none. You must do some different things and do some other things differently.

You must think up some new ideas, and you must be willing to think creatively!

Take out a piece of paper, write the desired outcome at the top, and start listing possible ways to get to the desired outcome. Do not edit out any ideas, but rather include all possibilities, even crazy ones, because sometimes they are the best ones. Think creatively like James Anthony Carter, the success coach, teaches his audiences to do. To think "outside of the box." Think possibilities and you will create new possibilities.

Be Resourceful: Sometimes You've Got to Improvise!

I think back to my days as a full-time singer. One night I was scheduled to play at a wedding. The piano player and the saxophone player were riding together and their car broke down. The reception was about to start and they were ready to announce the wedding party, and the band didn't have a piano or a saxophone player. What should we do? What could we do? I told the drummer and bass player to follow me, and I started singing the piano parts and adding little bits of saxophone sounds. I started improvising, and I created some sounds that sounded like instruments, à la Bobby McFerrin. I found that I had some skills I had never used before.

The crowd went nuts! It was an amazing night; and from that performance I was asked to do more and more music a capella. I started doing commercials and radio spots, with just my voice performing all of the instruments. In fact, on my last Music and Motivation CD, *It Only Takes a Minute to Change Your Life . . . The Music,* I performed a jazz version of "Blessed Assurance" where I sang over thirty individual parts. I learned that sometimes you have a challenge in life and you simply have to improvise. In doing so you will discover things that you didn't know about yourself. You will discover new possibilities for your life. What do you do when you don't know what to do? Improvise!

Turning Lemons into Lemonade and Turning Doggie Doo into Dollars!

On March 20, 1998, I read a wonderful story in the *Wall Street Journal* about turning lemons into lemonade or, to be more exact, about turning doggie doo into dollars. Diane Rossi was given up for adoption when she was seven years old and bounced around from home to home and school to school. She never even went to high school, and by the age of twenty-one was a divorced mother, was homeless and jobless and living in a car! While going through trash, she found a beat-up copy of a book called *The Magic of Believing: The Science of Setting Your Goal and Then Reaching It,* by Claude M. Bristol, that gave her a new perspective on life. She read the book and realized that she could make things better if she had faith and took responsibility for herself.

Diane got a job and struggled to pay for an apartment and childcare. One day she heard some of her neighbors arguing about who would clean up some doggy doo. She said, "I'll do it, if you pay me!" They did! She thought about it and decided to get some posters printed advertising this new service concept. She posted them around the neighborhood and the phone started ringing, and it kept ringing. In fact, it has not stopped ringing.

Diane Rossi has gone on to build a very successful company called "Have Doggie, We'll Doo!" She has a number of employees who ride around in her "Doggie Doo" vans, and she even started a national newsletter called *The Inside Scoop!*

There have been challenges and there have been problems, but she realized that opportunities rarely come in sweet, nicely wrapped packages. You must be resourceful and open to new ideas and you too can find dollars in nontraditional places. Keep your eyes open and use all of your stuff!

You must be resourceful and use all of your stuff, all of your talents and skills! Many of us have talents and skills that we never use. I remember when I was fired from my singing job and was completely down and out a friend told me to "use your stuff, use all of your stuff!" I was comfortable singing, but I was uncomfortable outside that arena; but at that moment I was hurting and needed to change my life immediately. I decided to leave my comfort zone and try some new things. I took a job with the school system and started a program called "Positive Images," using drama, music, and dance as a way to reach young people with a drug prevention message. I had never done any directing before, but it became a success and won a number of awards.

It was from that platform that I started speaking, again stepping out of my comfort zone. I had been a singer and that was all that I thought I could do and all I thought I could be. But I was willing to leave my comfort zone and try some new things. It was hard, it was difficult, it was scary, but I did it anyway. I started getting invitations to speak at schools to little kids, and then getting invitations to speak for teacher and staff in-service programs. I soon realized that I had some "stuff" that I had never used and probably would have never used, if I hadn't been pressed to try.

I remember one speech at an inner-city high school. This speech forced me to test how serious I was about leaving my comfort zone. Before the speech the principal asked, "Mr. Jolley, how long are you planning to speak?" I replied, "Oh, I usually speak about forty-five minutes." He quickly stated, "If I were you, I would speak about fifteen minutes. We haven't had much success with speakers who have spoken over fif-teen minutes!" As I waited to be introduced, I asked myself some hard questions. "Do I do what fear dictates or what faith dictates? Do I do what is comfortable or do what is necessary?"

Some of these young people had never heard a motiva-tional speaker. Some had never heard about the power of their dreams. Some were never told that they could achieve incred-ible things if they would commit themselves to excellence. I had to make a decision. I asked myself, "Should I tip-toe through the tulips and give a little fifteen-minute speech, get my check, and run off? Or should I step out on faith and share a message from my heart and overcome my fears? What should I do? What should I do?" As I stepped on the stage, I decided to follow my heart and do what was necessary, not what was comfortable. I started speaking. An hour and twenty-two minutes later, I stopped and sat down. . . . And the students gave me a standing ovation! That evidence taught me that you must be willing to do what faith dictates, not what fear dictates. Face the fear and lean on your faith. Most of all I learned that you must be willing to leave your comfort zone and use all of your stuff!

> *Most of us are standing in a river and dying of thirst.*
> —Cathy Mateo

If we would stop complaining and crying and start thinking about possibilities, we would begin to see that we have in-credible possibilities all around us. Incredible possibilities are within our reach. They are all around us. Yet so many of us are simply standing around crying and complaining about how bad life is. No! Stop and think! Be resourceful. Be proactive. Make it happen.

From Bankruptcy to Millionaire: What a Setback!

While speaking in Saint Cloud, Minnesota, I met a young man named Todd Russ, who told me about his brother, Dave, who turned a setback into a multimillion-dollar comeback. I told him I definitely wanted to talk to his brother. Todd arranged a meeting and the first thing Dave said was, "I don't consider my challenges setbacks; they are growth opportunities. If I had not had the setbacks, I would not have had this comeback!"

Dave had been in the tire business in the early 1980s and was having success. But in 1987, the bottom fell out and he lost all of his savings in a bad investment. Then a big order came in. But Dave didn't have the money to get the products, so he signed his personal resources as collateral. At the same time, as life would have it, the factory where he was to get the supplies filed bankruptcy and closed a week later! Due to the fact that he was personally tied to the shipment, he then had to file personal bankruptcy!

He struggled for about a year to regain the business but was unable to bring it back to life. It was a setback, but Dave continued to see it as a setup for a comeback. Dave decided to continue to do distribution, but started looking at other products. He didn't have credit, but knew the distribution business. So he got a partner, Mark, who did have credit. They developed a strategic alliance and started a company called Damark International Inc. Together they built a company that now distributes a number of products and is presently grossing over seven hundred million dollars a year and has over two thousand employees.

I asked Dave what was the key to this turnaround. He responded:

1. First you must decide whether you are going to live or die! Is this a setback or an opportunity to do something new?

2. Take action, big action, and look for new roads to your goal. Just because one street is closed doesn't mean there are no other ways to get to your goal.
3. Have faith! Faith in God, faith in yourself, and faith in the possibilities!
4. Remember that a setback is not the end of the world. It really is the start of a new beginning.

Realize that no matter what the problem is, you have something within you that is powerful and capable of turning the situation around, if you would just use it. It's in you! You are an incredible person, who has overcome other problems and challenges to get where you are now. Just remember how you got over those other problems. What did you do? Don't stand in the river and die of thirst. Drink in the possibilities. Drink in the positive energy. Drink in the victories. Drink in the resources. Drink, drink, drink in the wonderful possibilities all around you and start expecting them to become realities. It will take some new ways of thinking, and some reinventing; but like the caterpillar that becomes the butterfly, you too can fly.

An outstanding example of someone who reinvented himself is George Foreman, who holds the record for being the oldest person to ever become the heavyweight champion of the world. George Foreman grew up in Houston, Texas. During his teen years he was a big, wayward kid who became a boxer to keep out of trouble. He made the Olympic boxing squad of 1968 and won the heavyweight gold medal. He began a professional career in 1969 as a big, tough fighter who never smiled and had little personality. He dominated everyone he fought. He won the heavyweight title in 1973 by knocking out Joe Frazier. After that fight he was considered invincible.

However, in 1974 he fought Muhammad Ali in Zaire. And in

a daring strategic move, Ali used a new tactic called "the rope-a-dope strategy" to win the fight. It was George Foreman's first defeat; and he was devastated! He then went from bad to worse by losing another fight to a little-known fighter named Jimmy Young. This was a major setback! In the dressing room after that fight, George started acting strange and his trainers thought he was delirious, but George said he was having a religious experience. That night he quit boxing and decided to become a preacher. His boxing career was considered dead, and George Foreman was considered history; but he was not through making history.

George went back to Houston and started a church and youth center. Ten years later, after using all his own funds, he realized he needed money to keep the youth center alive, so he decided to go back into the ring. When he started this time, he was a changed person, a new person. He had reinvented himself. When he retired from boxing, he had been a mean, sulking, noncommunicative guy who just wanted to fight. When he came back he had been transformed, he was a new person. He was friendly, enthusiastic, fun loving, funny, and loved to talk.

His first fight after his comeback was in March 1987. He won that fight and kept going. He fought numerous times and won each time. He also was scoring a knockout punch with his new media image. He was quickly becoming one of America's favorite personalities and most popular commercial pitchmen. He sold everything from hamburgers to mufflers, and people loved everything he did. He won fight, after fight, after fight! In 1991, George lost a very hard fight to Evander Holyfield and many said that would be the end of the story for sure. He was over forty and overweight. All of the commentators recommended that George quit . . . he was just too old; but George had other ideas. He continued to fight and in November 1994 George startled the world. At the age of forty-five he won the heavyweight title of the world!

Not only did George win the title, but he also became one of America's most popular television personalities and product endorsers. He had made history as the oldest heavyweight champion ever! He has gone on to become a bestselling author, host of his own television show, and a high-demand public speaker. George Foreman is a man who reinvented himself and in doing so turned a setback into a setup for a comeback! I suggest that you consistently reinvent yourself and constantly stretch and grow. No matter how old you are, there is still a lot in you that is yet untapped and undiscovered. Keep seeking a new and improved you. There's a lot that you have left to discover. Seek it and you will find an improved you!

Be Smart!

Jim and Naomi Rhode are two friends who are members of the National Speakers Association. They have a tremendous story about turning a setback into a comeback. In the late 1960s Jim was the general manager of a small dental products company with his wife Naomi, as a dental hygienist. They had three small children and were struggling to make ends meet. The owner of the dental products company felt he was not making enough money so he decided to shut the operation down. If he shut down the company, Jim and Naomi would both lose their jobs. It was a setback, but it was not the end. Jim went to the owner and asked if he would be willing to sell the company to them. The owner laughed and said, "How could you buy this company?" But Jim persisted and finally the owner said, "Yeah, I'll sell it, but I doubt if you can afford it!"

Jim and Naomi collected all of their savings, mortgaged their home, cut back on all of their spending, and sold a lot of their possessions, yet they were still short by four thousand dollars! They went to the owner and asked for some time to get the money together. He refused! He wanted all of the money immediately and would not budge. Jim and Naomi called family and friends, but had no luck; finally they talked to the best man of their wedding, who also had a young family, and asked for his advice. It was in that moment that their lives changed. Their best friend said, "I really believe you guys are on to something. I'll find the money and you can pay it back whenever you can!"

That was over twenty-five years ago. Now they have paid that loan back with triple interest. Today Jim and Naomi are the owners of SmartPractice, a major dental products company in America, and have over three hundred employees. The company now grosses over fifty million dollars a year! Jim and Naomi proved that a setback is nothing but a setup for a comeback.

When I asked Jim and Naomi what the secret to their success was, they gave me a list that I want to share with you:

1. Keep a single purpose focus.
2. Keep a long-term view and think ahead.
3. Do not panic.
4. Develop a network and inventory your assets (hard as well as soft assets, like friends, family, your network, your talents, and your ideas).
5. Think possibilities and believe in the possibilities.
6. Conserve your money.
7. Always be careful with your "special team" (your family and loved ones, especially your mate).
8. Surround yourself with positive people.

9. Don't take rejection to heart. Every successful person has been rejected, and everyone started somewhere (everyone was once a rookie, a beginner).

10. Look at every problem as an opportunity, a time to try new things.

Ask! Ask, Ask!

When you have experienced a setback you must take a moment to look objectively at the situation. One of the best ways to do this is to ask questions. You must first ask questions of yourself; then you must ask questions of others. Finally, you must be willing to ask for help. At some points in our lives we will all need help.

When Faced with a Problem . . . Ask Questions!

One of the keys to success is to ask questions. You must ask lots of questions to not only figure out your options, but also to figure out what is the best move for you. First, ask yourself what are your options. Open your mind and start jotting down the answers. At first you might try to tell yourself that you have no options, like when people say, "I had to do it; I had no other choice." Friends, you always have a choice. It might not be comfortable, but you always have a choice. It's like in the pirate movies where the person is told to "tell where the buried treasure is or walk the plank."

Most times the person automatically says, "I guess I have to tell because I have no other choice." Well, they do have a choice . . . they could walk the plank. It might not be the easiest or most comfortable choice, but they do have a choice. It is possible they could walk the plank, fall into the water, and catch hold of a piece of driftwood. It is then possible for the person to hold onto that driftwood until it carries them to land. It might not be the easiest option, but you always have a choice. Remember, in life you always have a choice; it may not be comfortable, but you always have a choice.

Second, after you ask questions of yourself; then you must ask questions of others. One of the most important strategies for turning a setback into a setup for a comeback and achieving success is to ask lots of questions. Whenever I have a problem, I always ask questions of myself as well as others.

I ask myself for advice. I ask myself for advice and I recommend that you do the same. Ask yourself for advice! I say, "Willie, I need your advice. I have a problem, and I need your help. If you were me, what would you do in this situation?" I then proceed to give myself advice that I couldn't seem to come up with just a few minutes earlier. Why is that? Well, if a friend came to you for advice, even on a subject that you weren't an expert on, most people would try to help that friend. They would come up with some ideas and give some advice. I call that "brainstorming." And when you ask yourself questions, I call that "brainstorming with yourself." This means coming up with new ideas by asking yourself for advice, and allowing your mind to give you new ideas. Try it. It truly is amazing what creative ideas are already within you. You just need some new ways to tap into that great, unlimited pool of possibilities.

You also need to be willing to ask others for help. You must ask vertically and horizontally. To ask vertically is to ask upward, to ask help from God; and to ask horizontally is to ask sideways, to ask others. The Scripture says in Matthew 7:7 (RSV): "Ask and it shall be given unto you." And I love the old adage that "if you want to G-E-T, you must A-S-K! The same is true for turning your setbacks into setups for comebacks; you must ask.

This is a principle that can have a powerful impact on your ability to turn your setbacks into comebacks. Ask for help. Ask friends, family, associates, and even people you don't know. Ask for help, advice, information, and suggestions. You never know where you will get the answers, but you must ask the question in order to get the answers. Lee Iacocca was crazy enough to ask Congress for a loan to bail out Chrysler, and he got it! If you want to come back, you must be willing to ask for help, because you might just get it! You must ask questions and find answers as to what your options are. Before you do anything ask, "What are my options?" Once you know your options, you can then start to make definitive plans.

Even the Best Laid Plans . . .

I was scheduled to speak in Amelia Island, Florida, for a morning program. A few weeks before the program, I got a call from a friend asking if I would be the guest speaker for a celebration for the city of Ocala, Florida, on the evening of the same day. I told him that I was scheduled for Amelia Island in the morning and was available in the evening, so the only concern was getting from one city to the next. No big deal! Right? WRONG! Florida is a BIG state, and it happened that there were no flights going to Ocala that time of day. Plus it would take too long by car or bus. The people in Ocala really wanted me to come, so they offered to charter a private plane to pick me up. Great! I would love to ride on a Lear jet, but I was in for quite a surprise.

Finally, the day came and I finished my speech in Amelia Island. I stayed awhile, signed books and then got my bags and rushed out to the van that was waiting to take me to the airstrip to meet the private plane. We jumped in the van and started the trek to the airstrip. It took about twenty minutes, and I was right on time to catch my jet to Ocala. I was excited!

The driver dropped me off, unloaded my bags at the curbside, we shook hands, and said so-long. I ran into the terminal to meet the pilot and catch my plane. I told the lady at the counter my name and asked where I should go to get my plane. She said, "Not here! You're at the wrong place. The private airstrip is about a mile down the road." "What?!" I ran out to catch the driver, but all I saw of him was the back of the van as it faded into the distance. What do I do? There were no cabs and there were no cars. Just then a hotel shuttle van pulled up to get some cargo. So, I asked the hotel shuttle driver for help.

I asked the gentleman if he could help me get to the private airstrip down the road. I excitedly explained that I was late for a flight and had to get to Ocala immediately. He took pity on me and said, "Jump in." He took me to the next airstrip and dropped me off. I thanked him and ran in. I gave my name and told them I was there for the private plane. Everyone looked at me in a very strange way like I was speaking a foreign language. They said, "We don't have a private plane scheduled for you or anyone else today. What is the name of the airstrip where you are supposed to be?" I said Amelia Island. "Well, this is the Jacksonville airstrip. The Amelia Island airstrip is on Amelia Beach about twenty miles away." AHHHHHH! The driver had taken me to the wrong airstrip! I started asking questions again.

I asked about a cab, but they said it would take a half hour for a cab to get there. I asked about a rental car and again no luck. As I was going through my list of questions, a young pilot walked in and asked what was going on. We explained my predicament, and I asked, "Can you help me get to the airstrip, fast?" He said, "Well, I guess I could give you a quick ride over to the other airstrip in my plane. It should take about ten minutes to get there." "Great! Let's do it," and we went out to his plane.

Just as he was about to pull his plane out, he looked up and said, "The sky doesn't look too good; I think I'd better check the weather." He got on the phone and then I heard him say, "Uh-oh!" He turned to me and said, "There's a big storm coming in the direction that we need to fly into. I have a small, single-engine plane, and I cannot compete with that storm. Sorry, but I can't fly you there!" Again I started asking questions. I said, "Okay, what are my options? There are no cabs, no rental cars, and now you can't fly me there. Do you have a car?" He looked and said, "Well, I have a small car here on the property; I guess I could give you a ride over there." "Alright!" I said, "Let's do it."

He ran into the garage and came out quickly. . . driving a Yugo! It was the smallest car I had ever seen. It only had two seats and hardly any room for luggage. We squeezed my bags in the car, then we squeezed in and, gasping, I said, "Put the pedal to the metal," and he did, only for me to find out that the pedal to the metal was only forty miles an hour. I said, "Is this as fast as this goes?" He said, "Yep! Especially when the wind is pushing it!"

Finally we got to the Amelia Beach field, and my pilot was nervously pacing back and forth. I was over an hour late and there was a storm approaching. I thanked my Yugo pilot friend, gave him my card, a book, some tapes, and some cash for his time and energy, and ran up to greet the gentleman, holding a sign with my name on it. He was the pilot and said we had to go immediately because we had to beat the approaching storm. Even with all the challenges, I was excited! I had never been on a private jet, and I was ready for the experience. And I did have quite an experience in front of me.

We grabbed my bags and ran around the terminal and . . . I stopped and looked at what I was about to get into. It was not a Lear jet. It was a little teeny-weenie plane with two seats, two windows, and one propeller. In fact it looked like a Volkswagen with wings! If I'd thought the Yugo was a ride, I was in for the ride of a lifetime.

The pilot said, "Let's go. If we want to beat this storm, we've got to go NOW!" I got in and immediately started praying . . . out loud! I prayed my regular "Flyer's Prayer" (enclosed at the end of this chapter) and I started praying every prayer I had ever learned and some I didn't know.

I buckled up, held on, and kept praying, and we took off. The wind was blowing harder now, and the plane was struggling to gain altitude. Rather than going up, it seemed to be going sideways. The pilot was fighting with the controls, and I was praying. I kept thanking God for a wonderful and safe flight, in advance. The pilot kept pulling on the controls, and I kept praying and, and, and . . . and finally the plane rose above the storm and flew effortlessly above the clouds. It would have been a good time to make a rest room break, but as I looked around I realized there was no rest room, the only option was outside. I decided to wait! We got to Ocala about ten minutes after the program had started but right before I was scheduled to speak. And did I speak that day! I had a new attitude, and I was highly motivated!

I learned a lot that day about setbacks and turning them into a setup for a comeback. I learned about the power of asking. In retrospect, first I should have asked what was the name of the airstrip! Then I should have asked if the driver knew how to get there. That would have saved a lot of headaches. Next, I learned about asking about options, because there are always options. You just need to find out what they are so you can make a qualified decision. I also learned about asking for help, because as John Donne once wrote, "no man is an island," no one stands alone. Sometimes we all need help and we should not be ashamed to ask for help. Super successful people make a habit of creating a network of strategic alliances of people they know will be their support system. They know the importance of asking for help. Finally, I learned again that prayer truly is a powerful thing!

Don't be ashamed to ask for help, because sooner or later we all need help. As children we got help from our parents or guardians. They picked us up when we fell down, they dusted us off, and kissed our hurts away. As school kids we got help from teachers, who instructed us and directed us. As adults we get help from family and friends, who are there to hear about the problems and to help us up after life has knocked us down. Whether we call them parents, teachers, business associates, or mentors, whatever you call them, it still means the same thing—people who help! No matter where you are in life, there will be times when you will need help. Don't be ashamed to ask!

Step Six: Teaching Points:

1. Stop and think about your options.
2. Step back and get some space between you and the problem.
3. Check out the situation and "size it up"; then size it down by using limiting words like "just" and "only" to describe the problem.
4. Tap into your inner genius, your experience base.
5. Be resourceful; think outside the box.
6. When you don't know what to do, improvise.
7. Reinvent yourself; constantly stretch and grow.
8. Develop a network and create strategic alliances.
9. Do what is necessary, not what is comfortable.
10. Ask questions. Ask for help and ask about your options.

The Flyer's Prayer

Father, Thank You *for Another Opportunity to Fly* YOUR *Skies! I ask now that* You *take complete control over this plane and that* You *dispatch a legion of angels to cover this plane. From the front to the back, from the top to the bottom, from wing to wing. Let this plane go up at its appropriate time and come down at its appropriate time. With no incidents, accidents, or unplanned occurrences. And I pray that everybody on this plane will be Blessed. . . . Blessed because You reside in me and I reside in this plane. In the Name of Jesus I Pray. Thank You, AMEN!*

—Willie Jolley

◇ ◇ ◇ **Part Three**

The Power of Action

In the last chapter, we talked about the power of asking and how the Scripture of "asking, seeking, and knocking" teaches us about the power of asking. But there is also another teaching point that can be extracted from that Scripture, Matt. 7:7 (RSV) which is the importance of action: "Ask and it shall be given unto you, seek and ye shall find, knock and the door will be opened unto you. For everyone who asks, receives; and everyone who seeks, finds; and everyone who knocks, the door is opened unto them." Notice that each one of these points is connected to an action statement. If you take the action, then you will get the blessing. Most people receive not because they ask not, seek not, and knock not! Those who act are those who get. You must take action if you want to get results!

Step Seven

Take Action:
You Can Have Lights, You Can
Have Cameras, but Nothing
Happens Until You Take Action!

On the sands of hesitation, lay the bones of countless mil-
lions
Who at the dawn of victory, sat down and waited, and in
waiting died.

—Evangeline Wilkes

Sometimes you must fake it until you make it ... Act
yourself into a new way of thinking and think yourself
into a new way of acting.

—Willie Jolley

◇ ◇ ◇ The next key ingredient you need to turn a setback
into a setup for a comeback is action. A vision without action
is an illusion, and action without a vision is confusion. But action and vision, desire and decision, can change your life and
can change the world. Or, as Marlon Smith, the youth motivational trainer, says, "A vision without action is a wish, and
wishes have no substance."

Earlier, I talked about the fact that ants have an innate understanding of the importance of goals. They work hard and
persist to make their goals realities. Ants understand that hard
work is a critical element in the quest to reach your goals.

Hard work is the key. This is an excerpt from my book, *It Only Takes a Minute to Change Your Life* that speaks about hard work.

Hard Work Works

I received a call from my friend and attorney Amy Goldson, with a quote that she'd gotten from her mother that was very helpful in her quest to become a lawyer. The quote simply stated, "Hard work works!" And that is true! There is no substitute for hard work. Success is not the result of luck or good fortune, but rather of hard work and persistence. In Proverbs 28:19, 20 (RSV) it states that "hard work brings prosperity, while playing around brings poverty!" It might be uncomfortable, but it is absolutely necessary to work hard and persist, if you are serious about turning your setbacks into comebacks. "The only place where success comes before work is in the dictionary. William Penn wrote, "No pain, no palm; No cross, no crown; No thorn, no throne; No gall, no glory!" Janice Krouskop, author of *Happy Thoughts for a Healthy Life,* put it so well when she said, "Without ambition one starts nothing, and without hard work one finishes nothing. Therefore, those who stretch their backbone to reach their wishbone will make things happen!" I believe that says it all. First, there is the goal of what you want to achieve; then comes hard work, followed by determination and persistence.

Persistence and perseverance are essential elements in the quest to turn a setback into a setup for a comeback. It might seem like this ingredient goes without saying, but let me tell you it needs to be said over and over again. It needs to be said in the morning, at noon, and then again at night; in fact, it needs to be said during your dreams! Persist . . . never give up!

W. Mitchell exemplifies the power of decision and the

power of choosing success. W. Mitchell is a friend who constantly inspires me. I first heard about W. Mitchell via a Zig Ziglar tape. Then I heard Anthony Robbins talk about him and then many others after that. I first met him at the National Speakers Association and we became friends; in fact, he wrote the introduction for my last book. Mitchell is an inspiration because of his willingness to turn setbacks into comebacks over and over again. His story is legendary because he is a person who exemplifies turning setbacks into comebacks. He shows us the power of a P.H.D. Not a doctorate of philosophy but a doctorate of persistence, hunger, and determination.

The Man Who Would Not Be Defeated, W. Mitchell

W. Mitchell is a man who exemplifies turning setbacks into set-ups for comebacks. He is respectfully called "the man who would not be defeated" because he never gives up. Twenty-five years ago Mitchell was a student who worked part-time as a cable operator in San Francisco. Between school and work, he found time to ride his new Harley Davidson motorcycle for recreation. He lived for times when he could get out on his bike and feel the refreshing wind blow on his face.

One day while taking a ride, Mitchell was crossing an intersection and suddenly saw a truck running a red light. The truck slammed into him, and he was slammed to the ground. As he lay there in agony he smelled gas and realized he was covered with it. Suddenly there was an explosion and the bike went up in flames, and then the fire spread and soon engulfed Mitchell. He became a human torch and was completely burned from head to toe. He lost his fingers and toes and was left with no resemblance to his former self. He went through months and months of agonizing surgery and rehabilitation. He had a setback but he made a decision; he would not give up!

He finished his education and went on to start a business that soon became very successful. In fact, he was able to purchase a private plane that he piloted. His plane became his passion, and he spent all of his spare time flying. One evening, while in flight, the plane started experiencing engine problems. He attempted to land but lost control and crashed. When he awoke, after months in a coma, he found that now he was paralyzed from the waist down! He sat and looked at himself and saw a burned man who was now paralyzed and forced to live the rest of his life in a wheelchair. He had had a setback, but he decided not to give up!

Mitchell started saying, "You cannot control what happens to you but you can control what you do about it." He continued to fight for his dream and continued to make a difference. He has gone on to become one of the top motivational speakers in the world. He owns homes in Colorado, California, and Hawaii. He truly lives life to the fullest. He lives the life that he talks about. It's not what happens to you that counts; it's what you do about it!

You cannot give up; you have to fight on. You must make up your mind that giving up is just not an option. It must be a part of your make up, something that you have preprogrammed way deep down inside . . . giving up is not an option. I heard a person once say that "Nothing is stronger than a made-up mind" and I must agree. When you absolutely, positively make up your mind, you have created a powerful force. Resolve to become unstoppable.

Unfortunately, most people never really make up their minds. They think they might like to do something, but have not truly committed themselves. Therefore, they are easily swayed by the challenges and circumstances. Am I saying that if you make up your mind you are guaranteed to win in everything you do? NO! There are no guarantees in life; but I can say that if you give up, you are guaranteed NOT to win! If you want to overcome a setback and turn it into a comeback, you must make a predetermined decision that you will *not* give up! You just can't give up! As the advertisement says, "You've got to play to win!" That is also true in the game of life.

In order to overcome the challenging times and situations that life throws at you, it is essential that you make a predetermined decision to never give up. Those people who have turned their setbacks around always had a commitment to keep going. They decided that giving up was simply not an option. They went into the fight with confidence, determination, and persistence. Confidence came as a result of their belief in themselves. It was tied into their faith. They realized that faith is an essential part of every success story.

Mandela! Mandela!

When individuals rise above their circumstances and use problems to push them to become more, they grasp greatness.

—Nelson Mandela

Nelson Mandela is a legend in his own time and one of the best stories of someone who understood that a setback is nothing but a setup for a comeback. He was a young lawyer who was jailed because he refused to accept the apartheid system in South Africa. He was in jail for twenty-seven years and was consistently offered his freedom if he would make a public statement that he was accepting of apartheid, but he refused. The South African government offered him money and privileges, but he refused. Mandela was finally released after twenty-seven years, but that was not the end of this incredible comeback. First, he helped to orchestrate the end of apartheid in South Africa. A few years later, he became the first black president of South Africa! From prisoner to president! Oh, what a way to turn a setback into a setup for a comeback!

Know What Is NO!

Sometimes you will have setbacks when people slam doors in your face and tell you "NO!" Well, I say that a "NO" is nothing but a "Yes," waiting to happen. Sometimes people will just say no to you because they aren't sure how serious you are. Sometimes people will say "No" because that it is the easiest thing to say. People will say "No" and think that will get you to give up, which it does for most people. The achiever, though, doesn't let a "No" break their spirit. They understand that a "No" doesn't mean you should give up; it just means you must try again in a different way. They understand that persistence is the key to changing a "No" into a "Yes," because persistence always breaks down resistance! What is a "No?" It is nothing but a "Yes" waiting to happen. Is it a setback? NOOOO! It is just a setup for a comeback!

Determination is the next step. Many people get the words *determination* and *persistence* confused. They feel they are the same, yet they are quite different. Persistence is an action, determination is an attitude. Determination is the attitude that allows you to keep going in spite of the problems, in spite of the challenges. I have a quote above my desk that states: "The bulldog is one of nature's most determined creatures. The nose of the bulldog is slanted backward so he can continue to breathe without letting go!" We must be like the bulldog and simply never give up. Become confident, determined, and persistent, and learn to breathe without letting go!

I share with audiences that the key to success in any venture is just to keep going, keep trying. The old saying is true, that "winners never quit and quitters never win," and the real fact is that many times the only difference between a winner and a loser is that the winner just keeps trying. They may not have had any more talent or any more ability, but they just keep going. When the going got tough, they did not stop. Zig Ziglar has a saying: "The difference between a big shot and a little shot is a big shot is a little shot who just kept on shooting!" I truly believe that the key to success in any venture is to make a commitment to keep going. When you get your vision, you will also have opposition, and that is when you must persist and never give up!

Step back, take a deep breath, cry if necessary . . . but then get back up and get back at it.
　　　　　　　　　　　　　　　　　　　　　—Willie Jolley

Folks, we all get tired, and need to step back sometimes, but the winners get back into the fight quickly and keep fighting until they get what they want. Then they get ready for the next battle, because they understand that life is challenging and setbacks are a part of the challenge. They're a part of life! Know that tomorrow is a brand-new day and has brand-new opportunities. Along with the new day, winners realize that there will be new challenges, but they have developed the will to face each challenge as it comes. Scripture says do not worry about tomorrow's problems. Let tomorrow handle the problems of tomorrow. Focus on today, and enjoy the ride. As my friend Larry Winget says, "Expect the best, prepare for the worst, and celebrate it all!"

I Quit!

My son and I were riding by the place where I used to work as a drug prevention coordinator. My son was about six years old at the time, and he asked, "Dad, isn't that where you used to work?" I said, "Yes, it is." He then asked, "Dad, did you get fired or laid off?" I replied, "No, son. I quit!" As I said that, the tears welled up in his eyes and he said, "Daddy, you quit? You quit? But, Daddy, you told me never to give up; you said I should never ever give up. And you quit?" And as the tears rolled down his cheeks, I pulled the car over to the curb, wiped away his tears, and said, "William, I'm going to give you a life lesson, Son. See, yes I quit! But not because I was giving up! *I quit because I was going up!*" Friends, sometimes you have to quit those things that keep you down, you have to quit those things that make you frown, you have to quit those things that keep you bound. As my godmother in the motivation business, Rosita Perez, says in her speeches, "You must be willing to jump . . . and grow wings on the way down!" What is it in your life that you need to "quit" in order to go up? Sometimes you must change directions and strategies in order to reach your dream, but you must never stop trying. Remember, the magic of triumph is the first syllable . . . try.

Step Seven: Teaching Points:

1. Take action because a vision without action is a wish and wishes have no substance.
2. Hard work works.
3. Without ambition nothing gets started, and without hard work nothing gets finished.
4. It's not what happens to you that counts, it's what you do about it.
5. A "No" is nothing but a "Yes" waiting to happen.
6. Persistence breaks down resistance.
7. Be like the bulldog, learn to breathe without letting go.

8. Expect the best, prepare for the worst, and celebrate it all.
9. Nothing is stronger than a made-up mind, so, make up your mind!
10. Quit those things that keep you down, keep you bound, and make you frown.

Step Eight

....

Take Responsibility: Face It, Trace It, Erase It, and Replace It!

> *You may not be responsible for being knocked down, but you are responsible for getting back up!*
>
> —Jesse Jackson

◊ ◊ ◊ The next step in the process of turning a setback into a comeback is to take responsibility. This means to face it, trace it, erase it, and replace it. It doesn't matter whether you caused the setback, or whether it was thrust upon you, you must take responsibility if you want to turn it into a comeback! Why? Because it is *your life, and you must take responsibility for your life!*

I know some setbacks are so painful and so unfair that you want to run and hide. But when all is said and done the setback is ultimately your responsibility. And our response to the setbacks ultimately determines our direction in life. We may not be able to control or choose the circumstances but we can choose the response. A case in point is Mrs. Doris DeBoe, whom I wrote about in earlier books, who is a four-time cancer survivor. She cannot control the fact that cancer continues to appear in her life, but she decided to win in spite of the cancer. Her favorite saying is: "I might have cancer but cancer doesn't have me!" She has made a conscious decision to take responsibility for her challenges, no matter how they appear, and she has decided to win, and has beaten cancer four times. We must take the hand we are dealt and learn to win with it.

While some setbacks are things that happen to us that we cannot control, other setbacks are often the results of our choices. We participate in the creation of many of our setbacks. In other words, we "mess up" and created "self-made" setbacks. We all occasionally have lapses in judgment, make mistakes, make poor choices, and create our own setbacks. I don't know about you, but I have done some things that were just plain stupid and created some of my own setbacks. It was not my intention to create a problem, but the end result was a self-made setback. And it was my responsibility to fix it.

When we have setbacks due to our errors in judgment, we must be willing to accept the fact that we are part of the problem and therefore, must be part of the solution. We must take responsibility, face it, say, "I messed up," and go about fixing it. One of the best examples of someone who made a mistake and then took responsibility and turned it into a comeback is actress, singer, and former Miss America, Vanessa Williams. She understood that you truly can turn a setback into a comeback, if you are willing to face it, trace it, erase it, replace it, and take responsibility.

Vanessa Williams made history in 1984 when she became the first African American to win the Miss America crown. But less than a year later, the crown was taken away because it was discovered that she had had explicit photographs taken of herself during her college years. It had been a mistake, an example of poor judgment that came back to haunt her. It was a devastating setback. She lost her crown and her "girl next door" image.

She was disappointed, embarrassed, humiliated, but she was not a quitter. She disappeared for a short while and many thought that would be the end of Vanessa Williams. But they were wrong, she came back stronger than ever. She showed us that a setback really is nothing but a setup for a comeback.

What were the things she did in turning her setback into a comeback? The first thing she did was to pray, because she said, "When you pray, you find the answer." Second, she made the decision to hold fast to her dreams and never give up. She said, "The vision never changed. It was just set back a bit." Third, she realized that she still had talent, and she worked hard to showcase her singing and acting talents. She said, "It was not like my vocal cords were cut. It was a setback not a defeat, and I knew I still had talent!" She started recording beautiful love songs and became a bestselling recording artist, eventually winning an Academy Award for her rendition of the theme song for the movie *Pocahontas*. She then moved to television and the stage, even winning rave reviews for a starring role on Broadway in the hit play *Kiss of the Spider Woman*.

Vanessa went on to do movies. She started with small parts, but Hollywood soon realized she was a bona fide actress. She went on to become a box office superstar. She even starred with Arnold Schwarzenegger, who told her, "You are not just a survivor; you are a thriver. You showed the world that you are not just a pretty face, but you have guts, courage, and perseverance. You came back and proved you are truly a winner!" Vanessa Williams showed us that we all make mistakes, and our mistakes create some of our setbacks. But even those setbacks can be overcome, if you are willing to take responsibility.

Webster's defines *responsibility* as being morally, legally, and mentally accountable. I say that responsibility also means that you must respond with ability, all of your ability; in fact, to respond with all of your natural-born abilities. Earlier, I spoke of my friend Keith Harrell, and his Superfantastic Attitude! He shared a story where he was getting off a plane, on his way to a speech, and someone asked him, "Do you play with the NBA?" (Keith is six feet, seven inches tall and was a college basketball player.) Keith stopped, looked the person in the eye, and said, "Yes! I do play with the NBA . . . I play with my natural born ability, and I am slam dunking every day!" You too must respond to life with your natural born ability. You must play the game of life with all that you have, as hard as you can, and take responsibility for your success or failure.

Steps for Responding with Ability:

To take responsibility and respond with your natural born abilities, you need to employ four steps, which are:

1. Face It!

> *Face your problems and acknowledge them, but do not let them master you!*
>
> —Helen Keller

The first thing I do when I have a setback, a problem, a difficulty in my life is to face it and acknowledge there is a problem. Acknowledgement is the first step to resolution. If you act like an ostrich and stick your head in the sand, you might miss a few problems but you will also miss a great number of opportunities.

You cannot solve the problem if you don't accept that the problem exists. It's like the lady who didn't want to face the fact that her bills were more than her income, so she just started putting the bills in a dresser drawer and ignoring them. She figured they would go away. WRONG! She ended up with her wages garnished, a number of lawsuits, and a bad credit rating. You must be willing to face up to your setback if you want to turn it into a comeback.

The first step to recovery from anything is to first admit that there is a problem. Whether it is a drug problem, an alcohol problem, a sex problem, or whether you lost a job, or lost a loved one. You must face it so you can then look at the options, make appropriate decisions, take appropriate action, and move on. Remember, wherever there are challenges, there are always opportunities.

After acknowledging there is a problem, the next thing I do is pray. I told you earlier, when I have a setback I always take time to pray for wisdom and courage. I pray for wisdom so I can know what to do and courage so I will be strong enough to do what is necessary. And I do not always pray for God to fix it, but rather for God to help me face it, because I know if I can face it, then He can help me fix it! After I pray, then I know it is time to act, because prayer and action go hand in hand. First pray, then PUSH, which means Push (Take Action) Until Something Happens. You must take action. James 2:20 (KJV) says: "Faith without works is dead." Faith must be manifested in action. Therefore, you should pray like it all depends on God, and work like it all depends on you!

Dr. John's Story. Dr. John Pffeferle is a friend who exemplifies the power of prayer and action. Dr. John, as he is affectionately called, is a dentist whom I met when I spoke at a conference in Maui. He has one of the most successful pediatric dental practices in the country. Yet during a conversation I found that it had not been accomplished without some difficulties and without some pain.

Dr. John shared how he was just getting on his feet with his practice, he went to work one day and his number-one assistant came in and announced that she was resigning immediately. He was concerned because it was in the middle of

December, and his busiest time of the year. Kids are home for the holidays and parents are rushing to get all their medical needs met before the end of the calendar year.

As he sat and wondered what to do, his second assistant came in. He was glad to see her so they could discuss how to overcome this problem. To his surprise she too had an announcement; she was resigning also, and she was leaving immediately . . . to work for his competition. WHAT? An hour later his last employee came in and she too resigned. Dr. John had to make a decision, to either close shop or to keep going. Dr. John realized that he loved his little patients, and he decided that they were worth the fight. He fought on, and went on to build a practice that is now considered one of the most successful in America. Now he even goes to Third World countries once a year and donates his services.

Dr. John told me that the key to his success was a sincere love for his patients and a sincere love for dentistry. When his entire staff quit, he had to first look at himself and find out what he could do to better himself and then learn from the experience. Next, he decided to go on a program of self-development. He understood that the best way to build your future is to build yourself. He also realized that he needed to make training and development a must for himself and his staff. Love what you do, fight for it, and take responsibility, whether you created it or not. Build yourself and build you future.

When you are hit with a setback, make sure you are willing to look at yourself as well as the circumstances. And determine how you must change in order to create change! Take responsibility and remember, if it can be done, then it must be done!

Discover Your Strength! Cindy Jones is another great example of facing a setback and moving on to turn it into a comeback. In 1962, when Cindy Jones was a twenty-six-year-old housewife, her husband went to work one morning and never returned. The phone call from the hospital said he had been killed in an automobile accident. She was devastated. Her heart was broken; her dreams shattered. There was an overwhelming void in her life.

Four days later, Cindy went to the hospital and gave birth to her second son. She felt like she was living her life "out of sequence." Babies are supposed to be born long before their fathers die. In just a short time, the shape of her family had changed from two parents and one child to one parent and two children.

Fear consumed her! Fear of going on, fear of the relentless pain for which there was no relief. Nothing seemed safe or dependable anymore. But Cindy knew she had to face it; she couldn't just cop out! As the sole supporter of two children, she needed a career and a regular paying job. She had to face it, and she did.

Cindy made up her mind that she would take an active role in the rebuilding of her life rather than let things happen by chance. She wanted to make certain her life represented the best that was within her. That forced her to look deep inside, to find her own uniqueness, her own special attributes and abilities, inner strengths and talents.

A few months after her husband's death, Cindy took the money they had been saving for a new home and went back to school for a teacher's certificate. As a grieving widow and mother of two, she started classes on a cold January day at the University of Michigan. Walking into class the first day was extremely painful and lonely. She really struggled to push through her pain. She prayed for strength to continue to face it.

She went on to become a successful teacher, then a national speaker, and president of her own consulting firm. She faced her problems and was able to rise above her circumstances and overcome the challenges, even though they were initially bleak and life shattering. She found that the pull of the future was much more powerful than the push of the past. Finally, Cindy said she'd learned that life is much like a ten-speed bicycle—often we have gears we never use until we are forced to. We can all start using all our gears from wherever we are, with whatever challenges we have, but first we must face them.

2. Trace It!

Where did the problem originate, and what can you learn from the experience? To trace it you must look back and see what you can learn from the setback and also see if you had anything to do with creating the problem. Was there something you could have done differently? If so, you can learn from this and not make the same mistake twice (once is a mistake, twice is stupid). Sometimes it occurs in relationships. Many people have setbacks in relationships and then go back and make the exact same mistakes in the next relationship. Others get hurt and take the opposite extreme; they give up on love and relationships totally.

We should learn from our past experiences, not give up on relationships because of those experiences. It just means that you use better judgment and more wisdom in future decisions. There is an old tale about a little boy who smelled hot rolls in the kitchen and went to get one and touched the pan, which was still hot. He burned his hand and refused to touch any more pans, hot or cold, because he was afraid he would burn his hands. He missed a lot of hot, tasty rolls because of his past experience.

Wisdom would suggest that the next time he smelled the rolls and wanted a hot one he would test it before touching it, or get a pot holder or oven mitt so as not to burn his hand. But not give up on rolls. We must learn from our past experiences, yet we must not throw the baby out with the bath water. Don't give up on people or relationships because you once got burned. Don't stop enjoying life because you have a few bumps along the way. Life is for living, not for shrinking away! And the greatest mistake a person can make is to be so afraid of making a mistake that they do nothing! It's okay to make a mistake; just learn from it!

A reporter asked a bank president: "Sir, what is the secret of your success?"

"Two words."

"And, sir, what are they?"

"Right decisions."

"And how do you make the right decisions?"

"One word."

"And, sir, what is it?"

"Experience."

"And how do you get experience?"

"Usually . . . it's because of wrong decisions, if you learn from them. That creates experience."

Successful people learn from past mistakes and make adjustments for the future. If you don't learn from the past you can create a cycle of mistakes, which leads to you beating yourself up. This leads to lower self-esteem, which leads to negative feelings about yourself and your decisions, which leads to more bad decisions. Then you start the cycle over again with more negative self-talk and lower esteem and more bad decisions. STOP THE MADNESS! If you make a mistake, so be it! Learn from it and keep going.

Erase It!

After you have traced the problem and faced the problem, then you must erase the problem. Do not dwell on it, and do not beat yourself up. Learn from the mistake, make a commitment to do better in the future, and let it go! We all make mistakes, that is why they put erasers on pencils and delete keys on computers. The old saying goes: "Experience is the best teacher . . . but experience is usually the result of mistakes!" Forgive yourself and move on.

There are two types of mistakes: those that teach and those that destroy. We can either see those mistakes as learning experiences, or we can see them as death blows. We can see them either as our teacher or our undertaker. It is your choice! I recommend that you make them your teacher. Let them stretch you and help you to expand and broaden your horizons. Mistakes are a part of life and they can be a great teaching tool. But remember, the biggest mistake is to try not to make any mistakes, because then you are doomed to fail! Those who do nothing may not fail, but the only thing they succeed at is doing nothing and achieving nothing! As Edison said, "I didn't fail ten thousand times in making the light bulb; I found ten thousand new ways that didn't work!" And Albert Einstein said, "It's not a failure if you learn from it!"

No one great became great without making mistakes. Mistakes are a part of growth and are a necessary part of success. You cannot change what has happened in the past, but you can fix some of the things you have done in the past. One way to erase the problem is to go back and fix past incidents that have been bothering you. Then you can move on. If you have hurt someone in the past and you have not apologized, go back and apologize. If you borrowed from someone, then repay them. Fix the mistakes as best as you can; learn from your experiences and move on. If you need to step back and fix something, do it. You do not have to dwell there, fix it and move forward!

4. Replace It!

Once you have faced it, traced it, and erased it, then you must replace it. There will be people, places, and things in your life that just beg to be replaced. Do them a favor and grant them their wish; leave them alone and replace them. Replace the negative element with a positive element and move to a place of peace, purpose, and passion. Make a decision, choose to be positive, and focus on the positive rather than the negative.

Change your self-communication. Do not beat yourself up. Make a commitment to change your self-talk. No more negative communication. Your self-talk impacts your self-image and your self-image impacts your behavior, which then impacts your self-talk, and the cycle continues on and on.

Sweet Talk Yourself

To change your life you must change your communication and make it a point to have positive self-talk. "Sweet talk" yourself and speak positively about your life. Say good things about your life because there is power in words. Sticks and stones may break your bones . . . but words can break your spirit! Watch what you allow yourself to say to you and to others. First, speak well about yourself! Always say good things to and about yourself! Love yourself and be willing to tell yourself that you love you.

I tell students to be careful of conceit, yet that they should love themselves and feel good about themselves. I remember when I was young, one girl would say to another, "You think you're cute," and she would deny that she thought she was cute. As I got older I thought about it and realized how stupid that was, to deny that you can be cute. You ought to think you are cute; it is much nicer than thinking you are ugly. Do not accept anyone's opinion that belittles you. If God made you, then you are beautiful. Period!

In order to turn a setback into a setup for a comeback, you must take responsibility and respond with your natural born ability. You must see that with every burden there is a blessing, and with every blessing there is a burden; a burden of responsibility to face it, trace it, erase it, and replace it. Try it. You'll not just go through it, but you will grow through it.

Step Eight: Teaching Points:

1. You may not be responsible for getting knocked down, but you are responsible for getting back up.
2. Respond with your abilities, your NBA (natural born abilities).
3. Face it: Acknowledge the problem and pray not just to fix it, but to help you face it.
4. Trace it: Look at the problem and see if you had anything to do with creating it.
5. Learn from the problem: Once is a mistake . . . twice is stupid.
6. Erase it: Don't dwell on the problem; forgive yourself and move on.
7. Replace it: Exchange positive experiences and information for negative experiences and information.
8. PUSH: Push (Take Action) Until Something Happens!
9. Take responsibility: If it can be done, then it must be done.
10. Change your self-talk: Sweet talk yourself; speak well of yourself.

Step Nine

....

Harness Your Anger:
Use It, Don't Lose It!

Sometimes a success is a failure who gets mad! Angry enough to take action! It's all right to get angry; just don't let anger get you!

—Willie Jolley

◇ ◇ ◇ You have just had a setback. You are upset, you are angry, what do you do now? First, know that anger is okay. It's okay to get angry and be angry. But you must make sure to control the anger and not let it control you. Anger is a natural reaction; the key is how you respond to the anger. If you maintain control, you win; but if you lose control, you lose. Maintain control and use anger to help you focus your energies and focus your actions.

I am often asked what motivates me. I say it is the anger I had when I was fired from my singing job and how I vowed I would never go back. Every time I get tired, I think back to that job and how I felt when I got fired. I immediately get energized. In fact, I purposely remember how I felt when I got fired, so I can use that anger as a motivational force.

I often think back to that day and how I felt, and I get angry all over again. Not steaming mad, but angry enough to get up and get busy. Not seething mad, but just angry enough to stay up a little later and get up a little earlier. Not seeing red, but just angry enough to say, "I will never, ever go back," and then doing whatever I must to be able to back up those words.

If that meant I had to go in the office when I didn't feel like it, so be it. If it meant I had to make one more call, so be it. If it meant I had to write one more page when my fingers were tired and aching, so be it: whatever I had to do to make sure that I never had to go back. Anger, under control, can be a powerful motivational tool!

Most people get angry when they have a setback or when they are treated unfairly and are really motivated for a few minutes. Then they let the anger subside and they never harness its power. Anger is like a mighty rushing river that can generate enough power to light a city. Imagine if you had a river, but no one ever used the water for power. Wouldn't that be a waste? Well, anger also has power and can be harnessed and used to positive results, just like raging waters can be used for positive results. You must use it to build not to destroy, to lift up, not to tear down. Use your anger. Don't lose it or excuse it. Rather, diffuse it, so you can control it and harness it to help you reach your goal!

While anger used constructively can be a powerful motivator, anger used destructively can destroy your dreams and kill your opportunities. Some people use anger as a tool in business negotiations: They intentionally get their opponents angry in order to distract them and push them to react emotionally rather than logically. It becomes crucial to maintain your control because "he who loses his temper, loses the war!" Successful people learn how to control their anger and make it an asset rather than a liability.

Those Whom the Gods Wish to Destroy, They First Made Mad!

Euripides had a saying: "Those whom the gods wish to destroy, they first made mad," which is a statement of fact in many business dealings. Many people use anger as a negotiating tool. If they can get their opponent angry, they know they can get a tactical advantage because emotional opponents react rather than respond. An emotional person is not as clear and focused as a calm negotiator. It is critical that you are able to maintain control over your anger. The key to controlling your anger is discipline, because anger is danger without discipline. Cathy Hughes is an excellent example of someone who learned to use discipline to manage her anger and channel it for massive success.

Cathy Hughes was born into a prominent African-American family in Omaha, Nebraska. As she grew into her teenage years she became increasingly rebellious and angry. She started hanging out with the wrong kids and got pregnant. Her family was upset and Cathy was in great despair as to what to do. She decided to have the baby. When her son was born, Cathy said that was her defining experience. She knew she had made some mistakes; but she decided in that moment that she was going to make sure she gave this child every opportunity to be successful.

Cathy decided to get serious about her education, so she put herself through school by working as a radio salesperson. She got a reputation as an excellent salesperson and programmer. But she also had a reputation as someone who had a bad temper and would sometimes let her anger overshadow her business decisions.

She continued to ascend the ladder of success and eventually became one of America's top programmers. She even created the "Quiet Storm" concept that has gone on to be a big hit on stations across America. It was not long before she started dreaming about owning her own radio station, but many people laughed at her when she told them her dream. "You?" they would say. "You are struggling with raising that boy, you're Black, and you're a woman! And you're always losing your temper! Hah! You'd better stop dreaming." But Cathy didn't stop dreaming!

She was offered a management position at a small, new station, and a promise of part ownership, if she left her current position. But in the midst of the transition they reneged on the promise and implemented a change that required her to take a lower position and no ownership. It was a defining moment! She had to make a decision. Should she settle, or should she fight for her dream of owning her own station and making her own decisions? Cathy decided to fight for her dream!

Then the crucial test came when she tried to purchase her first station in 1987. At the last minute the bank that was to finance the acquisition reneged and insisted they would only fund the sale if they could decide on the format of the station. She was a great programmer but they felt they knew better. She became furious. The bank negotiators knew of her temper and were waiting for her to react emotionally. But she didn't. She paused, gathered herself, took control of her anger, focused her energies, maintained her composure, and was able to think clearly throughout the negotiations.

She skillfully negotiated the deal and got the money as well as the oversight to run the station the way she wanted. She went with her ideas. And within a short time her station was a success. Then she was able to buy another station! Then she bought another and another and another and another. Today Cathy Hughes is the CEO of Radio One, and is one of the top radio executives in America, with seventeen stations (and counting) across the country! Her son, the one she bore as a teenager, who helped change her direction from an angry girl to a focused young lady, is now the president of the company. Cathy Hughes learned how to control her anger and how to turn a setback into a setup for a comeback!

Sometimes anger is not only helpful, it is absolutely necessary. Some people do not get motivated until they get angry.

They need anger to push them out of the nest and make them fly. Sometimes we need to be filled with "righteous indignation." So angry that we just won't take it anymore. Because often, a success is a failure who finally gets mad. Angry enough to take action. Anger can be a great motivator.

I have a friend who worked for the same consulting company for a number of years. Her employers always treated her terribly. They totally disrespected her and belittled her. Yet she kept taking it because she was just too afraid to take a chance. Her self-esteem was so low that she started believing that maybe they were right! She had been waiting for a specific job appointment, and her employer had promised her the position. Therefore she continued to "hold on" and to take all kinds of abuse because she was trying to wait for the promised position. Finally, the job became available. She knew she was finally going to get her due, but she didn't get the job. They gave the job to the newest person on staff because they wanted to make sure they kept him happy!

My friend was livid. She was "fit to be tied." She became so angry that she was finally motivated to take action. She decided to quit and start her own competing business. She focused all of her energies on building the company and soon she had built a successful consulting firm. It was not long before she was able to catch up with her former company. Then she surpassed them. She continued to do so until she was able to purchase them. She learned to harness and focus her anger and realized that massive success really is the best revenge. As the old saying goes: "Don't Just Get Mad, Don't Just Get Even, Get Ahead!"

Doug Craig is a man I met while I was speaking in North Carolina who exemplifies this strategy. Doug is a very active member of his community and a very successful businessman. He was not always that way. Doug was born in a poor mountain area. As a young man he started working with a small rental company. He worked hard to establish himself and helped the company to have phenomenal growth.

Doug continued to work hard and become the general manager. Then the company underwent an ownership change. The new owners decided they didn't want Doug anymore, so they fired him. Doug was just a few years short of retirement. He was hurt, he was disappointed, but most of all he was ANGRY. He asked himself, "What is the best way to get back at that company?" And he responded, "Build a better company!"

Doug harnessed his anger and started working on his new business. First, he needed to raise money, so he struggled for months and was finally able to raise $38,000. Doug worked long hours to get the company up and going. Once he got started he encountered numerous obstacles and challenges; but he refused to give up. Every time he thought about giving up, he would just sit down and think back to the day when he'd gotten fired. He remembered the feeling, and rekindled the anger. He used his anger to get reenergized and remotivate himself. Seven years later he had built an extremely successful company. He shared the steps he used to reach his goal:

1. You must make a decision. You must decide whether to let the anger beat you up or build you up. He decided to use the anger, to harness and channel the anger, and to make it an ally rather than an enemy.
2. You must stay focused on your goal and never lose sight of the motivating factors that got you going in the first place.
3. You must love what you do. You must really love what you do because that may sometimes be the only payment you will receive as you work on your goal.
4. You must totally believe in your dream and be willing to put everything you have on the line. Doug says make

it more painful to fail than pleasurable to succeed. "Commit so much that you cannot afford to fail. You have to make it! NO other options!"

5. Give your customers more than they paid for. Beat the competition with outstanding customer service, because it will always pay terrific dividends.

6. Have great faith in God! Trust and believe, and then act on your belief!

How did Doug turn his setback into a comeback? By turning his anger into a positive motivating force rather than a negative destructive force. Don't get mad, (because to be mad means that you are out of control), don't get even (because to get even is to be vengeful, or full of revenge, which is a negative emotion), no, get ahead! Let your anger motivate you to get ahead, because getting even is not good enough! Remember, massive success truly is the best revenge!

Anger Exercises

What things have made you angry? What things have made you mad? Do you want to get even or do you want to get ahead? If you only get even, then you are wasting a great opportunity and you are still thinking small and letting petty things cloud the big picture. Here are five strategies to help develop the discipline to control your anger and make it a productive rather than a destructive force in your life.

Develop a Pattern Interrupt. You must break the pattern of anger and establish a personal pattern interrupt. A pattern interrupt is something you do every time you feel your anger coming on. You can count to ten, take a quick walk, breathe deeply five or six times, or meditate and say a short prayer. Whatever you choose, you must have the discipline to use new behaviors to diffuse the anger and maintain clear thinking.

Ask Yourself Questions. After you calm down by using the pattern interrupt, you must ask yourself a series of questions: "Will this make a difference in a year?" If the answer is no, then "let it go!" If the answer is yes, then ask, "Can I control the time? No! Can I control the weather? No! Can I control what others say or do? No! What is the one thing I can control? Me! Then remind yourself of your goal. Ask, will the actions you are about to take help or hurt my goal?

Transfer the Emotion, Diffuse It, and Use It. Think of your anger as a stick of dynamite that can be very destructive if used at home but could be very helpful if used to gain access to a mountain of granite. Transfer the power of the anger so it will not destroy your home or your relationships. Then use the anger to open access to those mountains of granite that have kept you from achieving your goals.

Think Before You Act. "I'm so mad I can't see straight." Or, "I was so mad I didn't know what I was going to do." These are both statements of truth. And you should not do anything while you are not able to make clear and deliberate decisions. Do not say anything or do anything until you have collected your thoughts because words and actions expressed in anger are often those that are regretted most.

Remind Yourself of Your Goal. Focus on the goal and what you're trying to achieve and gather the energy that is generated from the anger to create an "I'll show you" attitude. Remember that you cannot control what happens to you, but you can control what you do about it. Don't just get even, get ahead!

* * *

When you have a setback do not forget it. Do not forget the event that originally caused the anger. Capture the moment and remember the feeling and use it as a motivational tool. Like a friend who keeps a paperweight on her desk from the company that fired her. She keeps it right in her view to keep her motivated when she has challenging days.

In the 1800s, "Remember the Alamo" was the rallying cry of the Texas patriots who refused to forget the massacre at the Alamo. Even when they were outmanned, they were able to reenergize themselves when they brought back mental pictures of the Alamo through the battle cry. They beat bigger foes and overcame impossible odds because they had anger and righteous indignation. They reminded themselves to never forget the Alamo!

Anger can be rekindled time and time again. It can help you to win against all odds, beat giants, and overcome impossible situations. Remember your anger, and remember how you felt. Use it over and over again to reenergize yourself. Anger . . . harness it and use it, not to get even but to get ahead. Remember MASSIVE SUCCESS truly is the best revenge!

Step Nine: Teaching Points:

1. Sometimes a success is a failure who finally gets mad. Angry enough to take action.
2. Don't just get mad, don't just get even . . . get ahead.
3. Control your anger, remember those whom the gods wished to destroy, they first made mad.
4. Danger without the *d* is anger, which stands for discipline.
5. Make anger an ally rather than an enemy. Use anger as a motivational tool. Don't lose your anger, use your anger.

6. Remember, massive success is the best revenge.
7. Develop an anger routine to stay calm and collected.
8. Develop a pattern interrupt when you feel your anger is about to erupt.
9. Think before you speak and act.
10. Remember your "Alamo" and call on it often to stay motivated.

Part Four

The Power of Desire

The last part of the VDAD formula is desire. It is absolutely necessary in turning your setbacks into comebacks. When we hear the word *desire,* we usually think of things that we crave, but there is much more to desire. Yes, desire does have a definition that includes cravings and satisfying appetites. Desire also includes those things that you earnestly long for, and the degree of intensity that you are willing to exert in reaching the goal you have set. It is even the degree of energy you are willing to expend in reaching your goal. In other words, how badly do you want to reach your goal; and what are you willing to do in order to achieve it?

You must want to turn the setback into a setup for a comeback, and you must want it badly. How badly do you want to turn your setback into a setup for a comeback? Whenever I ask that question in my programs, I always get the same answer, "Real bad!" Okay, but how bad is "real bad?" There are different levels of wanting something "real bad."

Have you ever awakened late at night and had a desire for something to eat, or drink? We have all probably had that feeling at some point in our lives. Imagine a person who wakes up around midnight and says, "I want a soda and I want it real bad!" The person goes to the refrigerator and looks, but there are no sodas. They go to the window, open the shades, and see that it's snowing. They go back to the refrigerator and look again, but there are still no sodas there. So they settle for a glass of water and go back to bed. They really didn't want it that bad!

Another person wakes up around midnight and says, "I want a soda, and I want it real bad." This person goes to the refrigerator and looks, but there are no sodas. They go to the window, open up the shades, and see that it's snowing. They put on their hat, coat, gloves, and boots and walk a quarter mile to the corner store, but it's closed! So they walk back home and settle for a glass of orange juice. They really didn't want it that bad!

Another person wakes up around midnight and says, "I want a soda, and I want it real bad." This person goes to the refrigerator and looks, but there are no sodas. They go to the window, open up the shades, and see that it's snowing. They put on their hat, coat, gloves, and boots and walk a quarter mile to the corner store, but it's closed! They walk another mile to the gas station, with the soda machine, but it's sold out. But that person keeps walking and trying, and walking and trying, and walking and trying until they find a soda! Imagine if you would go that far for a soda, how much further would you go for your dreams? That is a question only you can answer! How badly do you want it?

Desire is broken down into three parts: (a) the desires of your heart, which are determined by your faith; (b) the desires of your mind, your level of focus, and your commitment to achieving your goals; and (c) the desires of your soul. This is your insight and attitude toward the setback and how serious you are about turning the setback into a setup for a comeback.

Let's start with the desires of your heart, which are determined by your faith. Faith is absolutely necessary in your quest to turn a setback into a comeback!

Step Ten

Have Faith: "You Are Blessed
and Highly Favored!"

*If you can just believe. All things are possible to them that
believe!*

—Mark 9:23

He who loses money, loses much
He who loses a friend, loses more
He who loses faith, loses all

*We go through life with a series of God-ordained opportu-
nities, brilliantly disguised as challenges.*

—Charles Udall

◇ ◇ ◇ While I feel that all the chapters of this book are important, I truly believe that this is the most important chapter.
Because faith is critical to turning a setback into a setup for a
comeback. Faith is critical because it gives hope; and hope
gives us an optimistic expectation for the future. With an optimistic expectation of the future, we are more apt to keep going in difficult times. If we are able to keep going in difficult
times, then we will be able to effectively turn our setbacks into
comebacks over and over again.

Faith gives us hope, and faith also gives us strength. It is a
power source that allows us to keep striving, specifically in
tough times. And since we now know that we will all have
some tough times, we need faith. And everyone has some
faith. The question is: Where is your faith?

See, everyone has faith. Unfortunately, some have misplaced their faith. I know everyone has faith because I have studied people as they go through their daily routines. I've seen how they applied their faith. Like the person who walks into a restaurant, pulls out a chair, and sits down, without checking to see if the chair can hold their weight. They have faith that the chair is able to do what it is was created to do. Or, the people who get on an airplane and take a seat, without asking to see the pilot and checking his or her license. We have faith that the airline would only have a qualified, experienced person in the position of pilot. Another example is when people get a job and work for two weeks or even a month without any money from their employer! They have faith that the person will pay them at the appropriate time and that their check will be good. Faith! Everyone has faith!

Yes, everyone must have faith in order to exist in the world as we know it. But where is your faith? That's a powerful question that must be answered whenever you have a setback and want to turn it into a comeback. Where is it? Is it in the problem, or is it in the solution to the problem. Is it in the present circumstances, or is it in your future possibilities. Is it in your fears or is it in your faith? Is it in Murphy's Law, or is it in God's promises? Where is your faith? I say have faith in a God who will help you to understand those things that others mean for bad, He means for your good. Have faith in a God who can truly help you to see that a setback really is nothing but a setup for a comeback.

Joseph and the Coat of Many Colors

The biblical story of Joseph is one of the best stories ever about the power of a setback turning into a comeback. Joseph was a young man who was a dreamer. He was his father's favorite son. He was given a coat of many colors. Joseph would share his dreams with his brothers, and they hated him because his dreams always showed him rising above them. One day they decided to get rid of this "dreamer" once and for all. When Joseph came out to the field, his brothers threw him into a deep pit. They had planned to kill Joseph. They took off his coat of many colors and threw animal blood on it, so they could take it back to their father and say that Joseph had been killed by a wild animal. While they were trying to decide who best to kill him, a band of traders came along. The brothers quickly sold Joseph to the traders. Joseph had a setback, a big setback!

The traders took Joseph to Egypt and sold him to Potiphar, who was an officer of Pharaoh, the king of Egypt. Joseph flourished as Potiphar's assistant, and everything he touched became a success. Soon he was put in charge of all of Potiphar's administrative affairs and became Potiphar's favorite servant, but there was trouble brewing.

Potiphar's wife had romantic eyes for Joseph and consistently tried to seduce him and get him to sleep with her. Joseph consistently refused. One day, when everyone else was out of the house, she caught Joseph by his robe and insisted that he sleep with her. He ran but she got angry and started screaming and accused Joseph of attempting to rape her. Potiphar believed her story and threw Joseph in jail. This was another setback for Joseph, but God knew a comeback was on the way!

While in jail Joseph became friendly with the chief jailer, who made him his main administrator. The chief jailer gave Joseph responsibility over all of the other prisoners. Joseph became friends with two other inmates from the palace, the chief baker and the chief butler. One night they both had dreams that they could not understand, so they asked Joseph to interpret the dreams. He told the butler that he would regain his stature in Pharaoh's household. Then the chief baker got excited and asked what his dream meant. Joseph told him that his dream meant that he would be killed. It turned out that Joseph's predictions came true. The chief butler promised Joseph he would remember him when he was back in Pharaoh's house and would get him out of jail, but . . . he didn't, we forget! Another setback for Joseph.

Still Joseph never lost his faith. He believed something good would come from all his misfortunes. He continued to see a setback as nothing but a setup for a comeback. A few years later Pharaoh had a dream that none of his staff could interpret. Then the chief butler remembered Joseph. Pharaoh sent for Joseph and told him about the dreams. Joseph not only was able to interpret the dreams, but also gave him an action plan to overcome the challenges that were to come. The king was so taken by Joseph and his faith that he made him his personal assistant. Within a short time Joseph was promoted to be director of all administrative activities in Egypt and then became Pharaoh's second in command. At the age of thirty, Joseph became the second most powerful person in Egypt and had control over all the allocations of property and supplies.

Joseph had predicted seven prosperous years that were to be followed by seven lean years. He instructed the Egyptians to store food and supplies during the seven prosperous years in anticipation of the seven lean years. During the seven prosperous years, Joseph's stature continued to grow, as did his faith. Following the seven prosperous years, there was a famine, but the Egyptians had plenty because of Joseph's plan. The people in other neighboring countries were hit hard and many were on the brink of starvation. Joseph's brothers heard there was food in Egypt and decided to go to Egypt and try to buy some food there.

During this time Joseph was the governor of all Egypt. He was in charge of the sale of grain. Therefore the brothers had to come and bow before Joseph in order to get grain and supplies. Joseph recognized them, but they did not recognize him. He interrogated them and found out that their father was alive and well. He also found out that he had a new, younger brother. He finally told the brothers who he was, and told them to go get their father and move their families to Egypt so they could have food and provisions during the famine. Joseph forgave them for selling him into slavery because he said it was that act that had eventually saved their lives. He told them that what others meant for bad, God meant for good. He showed them that a setback is nothing but a setup for a comeback, but you've got to have faith.

To really become empowered to turn your problems around, you must have faith, faith in a God who will never leave you nor forsake you. This story is one of my favorites: the fact that you are never alone if you just have faith.

The Country Doctor

Once there was an old country doctor who lived in a rural area. He would go from farmhouse to farmhouse taking care of the people and their illnesses. One day in the middle of summer his car broke down and he had to walk from farmhouse to farmhouse. At the end of that day he was so tired he could hardly put one foot before the other. He wearily came into his house and was so tired he didn't even want dinner; he just wanted to go to sleep. He went into his bedroom and lay down and was asleep before his head hit the pillow. His wife came in and loosened his tie and unlaced his shoes and put his feet up on the bed.

About an hour later the phone rang, and the doctor's wife answered it so it would not disturb the doctor. It was Mrs. Smith from the farmhouse down the road. She was hysterical because her baby had a high temperature and she didn't know what to do. She needed the doctor right away. The doctor's wife told her that the doctor was too tired to come right now, but to give the baby a cold compress and aspirin and the doctor would be there first thing in the morning. Even though the doctor was in a deep sleep, his subconscious recognized that there was someone who needed him. He wearily said, "What's wrong?" His wife told him about the baby with the high temperature. Doc got up and said he had to go tend to the child.

He got his satchel and started to walk to Mrs. Smith's farm, which was about two miles away. To get to the farm he had to go through a tunnel. As he entered the dark tunnel a voice shouted out to him, "Hey, you got a match?" The doctor stopped and put down his satchel; pulled out a match; held it up close to the man's face so he could see it; struck the match, lit the man's cigarette; pulled the match back, and blew it out.

Doc proceeded on to Mrs. Smith's house. He worked on the baby and was able to get her temperature down and gave her medicine to make her feel better. He then started back on his trek home. When he got back to that tunnel, he again encountered a man in the midst of the darkness. The man again shouted, "Hey, you got a match?" Again the doctor stopped and put down his satchel, pulled out a match, held it up close to the man's face so he could see it; struck the match; lit the man's cigarette; pulled the match back, and blew it out. He hurried home and again fell into a deep sleep.

A few hours later the phone rang again. The doctor jumped up and caught the phone and gasped as he heard the information on the other end. It was the sheriff, who said that Mr. Brown, one of the doctor's best friends, had been walking through the tunnel that night when someone had jumped him, beaten him, robbed him, and left him for dead. He needed the doctor immediately if Mr. Brown was to be saved. The doctor quickly got his satchel and ran to the infirmary. He worked feverishly on Mr. Brown and was able to stabilize him so that they could get him to the hospital.

The doctor asked the sheriff, "Did you find who did this?" The sheriff said, "Yes, we have him over at the jail!" The doctor said, "Can I see him?" The sheriff said, "Yes," and took him over to the jailhouse. When they got there the doctor was astonished because behind the bars was the man he had encountered twice that night. The doctor went up to the cell and asked the man, "Why? Why didn't you hurt me?" The man replied, "It was my plan to not only rob you and beat you, but to kill you and steal all of your expensive medicines . . . but every time you lit the match . . . there was somebody standing next to you!"

Friends, you will have all kinds of encounters as you go along the way to do that which you have been commissioned to do. Some of these encounters will be frightening and painful and difficult. Yet you must always stay faithful and remember that we have a promise that God will never leave you nor forsake you. He will always be beside you. Just have faith.

So what is faith? Hebrews 11:1 (RSV) tells us that "faith is the substance of things hoped for, the assurance of things not seen." Scripture also tells us: "For God has not given us the spirit of fear, but of power, and love, and of a sound mind." Unfortunately, most people live their lives with a spirit of fear and not a spirit of faith. They allow fear to rest, rule, and abide in their lives. They live their lives with fear at the helm and faith as a stowaway. Live your life with faith at the wheel, and I suggest that you cast fear overboard.

Psychiatrists have proven there are only two fears that we were born with: the fear of falling and the fear of loud noises. Every other fear is a learned behavior. Babies come to this earth with only those two fears and then are taught the others. My friend, Dale Smith Thomas, shares in her speeches the meaning of FAITH versus FEAR! FEAR stands for false evidence appearing real, while FAITH stands for finding answers in the heart! What are the answers you will search and find in your heart?

Evander Holyfield, the Heart of a Giant . . . the Faith of a Champion!

Evander Holyfield is a person who turned a setback into a comeback by applying his faith and finding the answers in his heart. In 1994, Evander Holyfield lost his heavyweight title in a twelve-round decision to Michael Moorer. He was devastated because he had worked so hard to become the heavyweight champion. In addition to losing his title, he soon found out that there was another, bigger problem. He was diagnosed with a serious heart problem and had to retire from boxing.

Within a few weeks he had not one, but two major setbacks. Yet he had great faith and believed he had some great accomplishments yet undone. It was at a revival that he had his defining moment. During a revival in Philadelphia, he was told that not only would he return to the ring but he would also have incredible success. It was in that moment that he decided to rely on his faith. And it was in that moment that he changed his life and changed the boxing industry.

He decided to concentrate on the solution rather than the problem. He could have given up and retreated, but he had the heart of a champion. He focused on his faith and believed that these setbacks were just a setup for a bigger comeback. Most people counted him out and said he was finished, but he believed that bigger and better things were on the horizon.

Evander focused on his faith, went back to his vision, and then made the decision to make his situation a plus, not a negative. He worked on his health and continued to pray. He focused all of his energies on his health and his faith. It was not long before his heart diagnosis had changed and his heart was given a clean bill of health. Then he looked at his goal. He wanted to be the heavyweight champion of the world again. He looked at what actions needed to be taken and who he had to fight. Finally, he asked himself, "How badly do I want it?" He had to ask the question because he knew in order to reach his goal he had to fight Mike Tyson, the baddest, toughest fighter on the planet.

The fight was scheduled and all the media and all the pundits said that Evander Holyfield was going to get killed. But Evander refused to believe what others said. He continued to rely on his faith. He read the story about David and Goliath over and over again and found that anytime you have God with you, you immediately become a majority. He went into the fight with a dream and great faith, while Mike Tyson was vowing to knock his head off. He fought and fought and fought; and when the fight ended, Evander Holyfield was still standing and Mike Tyson was lying on the canvas.

Evander Holyfield had done the impossible. He had overcome a life-threatening heart problem. And he had gone on to beat Mike Tyson, who was thought to be "the baddest man in the world." Was it incredible? Yes! Was it impossible? No! Those who have great faith realize that with God all things are possible! Setbacks? Yes, but they are nothing but setups for comebacks. Where is your faith? In the fear in your head or the faith in your heart? The heart is the spot to change your fears into faith!

The Famous Wally Amos!

Wally Amos has become a friend over the last few years. We have spoken on a number of programs together and found that we have a lot in common. Wally is a great example of someone who turned a setback into a setup for a comeback. His story is legendary and has come to be a standard of never giving up.

Wally Amos was born in Florida and grew up in New York. As a young man he became interested in the music industry and became a music agent with the William Morris Agency. He quickly became a very successful agent. After his career at the William Morris Agency he formed his own personal management company. It was during that time that he began baking chocolate chip cookies and giving them away as a way of bringing attention to his clients. Ultimately, he decided to do what he loved and started a company called The Famous Amos Chocolate Chip Cookie Company.

He worked hard and in a few years people all over the country were buying Famous Amos chocolate chip cookies in stores across the country. He was a star! He started giving speeches and traveling and left the cookie business to run itself. Unfortunately businesses don't run themselves. They are like cars; they must have a driver or they will run off the road. The business got into financial difficulties so Wally started to look for a way to let someone else drive the runaway car. A company offered to buy the Famous Amos Chocolate Chip Cookie Company and keep Wally as the spokesman. Wally sold a major interest in the company.

Things were great for the first couple of months; then the company was sold to another company, who then sold it to another company, who then sold it to another, bigger company. By the time it got to the fourth owner, they felt they didn't need Wally anymore and told him good-bye. Then to add insult to injury they told Wally that he couldn't use the name "Famous Amos" anymore.

Wally told them that Famous Amos was his name, and people around the world knew him by that name. Wally and the company ended up in court, and Wally lost. He had to give up the name Famous Amos and could not even use it on any promotional materials.

He was down, but he was not out. Wally knew that a setback is nothing but a setup for a comeback. Wally told his family that God is not a one-idea God. He said, "God gave me the first idea, and I am confident that He will give me another." Wally soon got another idea and started a new company called Uncle No-Name's Cookies Company. He also became a bestselling author and media personality and developed an infrastructure that allows him to speak and travel while people he trusts are driving the business. Yet, proving truly that a setback is nothing but a setup for a comeback, Wally has recently been asked to rejoin Famous Amos as their spokesperson. He has been given a nice contract, plus he has received the rights back to his name. So he has now changed the name to his new company from Uncle No-Name's to Uncle Wally's. He now not only sells cookies but also sells fat-free muffins. He has gone from one company to two companies and a thriving speaking business. All because he kept the faith and turned his setback into a setup for a comeback!

Wally's steps to turn a setback into a setup for a comeback are:

1. Remember, God is not a one-idea God. If he gives you one idea, He can and will give you another.
2. Remember, God is greater than any situation you have. Have faith!
3. Always look for ways to turn lemons into lemonade.
4. Keep in mind there are no facts on the future. You create the facts!
5. It really doesn't matter where you came from, the key is where you are going.

6. Wally says, "I reached for the sky, but missed . . . so I grabbed a few stars."

7. Have faith, which is stepping out on nothing and believing you will land on something. Focus is directing your energies on a project and creating a fire. Follow-through is taking consistent, persistent action and making your dreams come true.

8. Wally proved that even a man with no name can turn a setback into a setup for a comeback.

Yes, I'm "Blessed and Highly Favored!"

In my first book I spoke of Zemira Jones as the man who first introduced me to the phrase, "Blessed and Highly Favored." When I first met Zemira, I asked him, "How are you?" And he responded, "Blessed and Highly Favored!" I said, "What was that?" Again he said, "Blessed and Highly Favored!" I told him that was a fantastic greeting and asked if I could use it and share it with others. He said, "Please, and share it a lot and help others see the power of positive affirmations!"

I have since made it my favorite phrase, and it has had a powerful impact on my life. In fact, it has become a mantra of sorts for me. I have had incredible experiences with overcoming challenges by using it as a daily affirmation. I now share that greeting with people all over the world. I say, "First state it, then live it! Blessed and Highly Favored!"

We now have a "Blessed and Highly Favored Club" with "Blessed and Highly Favored" T-shirts, hats, buttons, bumper stickers, a telephone line, a newsletter, a Web site, a travel group, and a music album. None of which would have ever occurred if I had not met Zemira Jones and simply asked him, "How are you?" The most interesting thing about Zemira Jones is not that he says he is "Blessed and Highly Favored," but more so that he lives it in his daily life. He has an incredible story that documents why he truly is "Blessed and Highly Favored!"

Zemira Jones grew up and went through school in suburban Washington, D.C. He went on to the University of Maryland, where he majored in marketing and business. He graduated from college and went into the radio business. After working for a small station in Baltimore, he got promoted and went to Cleveland. In a short time he rose to become the youngest general manager the station ever had. Meanwhile, he had gotten married, and his wife became homesick and wanted to go back to the Maryland area. So Zemira went to the owner of the station and asked if he could move to the sister station in Washington, D.C. The owner agreed but didn't have a GM position available so Zemira would have to take the job of general sales manager.

Zemira took the job and remained in that position for a number of years, growing the sales operation and waiting for his turn as GM. In the meantime, he also doubled in programming, and created a format called "Cool Jazz," which has since gone on to become one of the most popular formats in cities around the country.

He was extremely successful in every aspect of his job and was told that he would definitely be the next general manager when the spot was open. In early 1992, the opportunity came when the general manager retired. Zemira was ready for the job, but behind his back the position was given to the president's best friend. The new GM was told that Zemira had been promised the position and was not happy so he fired him! Rather than have any competition he felt it best to get rid of Zemira.

Zemira sat down and looked at the time he had invested, the promises he had waited on, and the sacrifices he had made to help build the station. He was crushed, but he was still

Blessed and Highly Favored! He sat down and made a list of the top five radio stations in the country and decided he was going to work for one of them.

He applied, but the only openings they had available were as starting salespeople. If he wanted to work at the station, he would have to start in an entry-level position as a salesperson. He would literally have to go from being a general to a buck private. Zemira decided to take the job! It was a setback! A major setback! He reminded himself, "Don't worry and don't fret! I'm Blessed and Highly Favored, and on that I will bet."

His friends in the radio industry thought it was an embarrassment. Some even laughed, but he kept saying, "I'm Blessed and Highly Favored! I'm Blessed and Highly Favored! I'm Blessed and Highly Favored!" He jumped in and went to work with the same energy and enthusiasm he had had when he was at the top. He truly believed in himself and was willing to bet it all on that belief.

He quickly became the top salesperson and within three months was promoted to sales director. He continued to set a record sales pace. In six months he was promoted again, this time to general sales manager. He went on to create record profits for the station. He continued in that capacity for a couple of years, constantly setting new sales records. Then one day, the president of ABC Radio called to congratulate him. He wondered if Zemira was willing to take on one of their biggest problem spots, the ABC affiliate in Chicago, which had sunk to last place in a very competitive market. Zemira said, "Sir, I don't see it as a problem spot; I see it as an opportunity spot!"

Zemira set out to build the station, against the odds, but with a strong confidence that he was "Blessed and Highly Favored." A year later it was in the top five in the market, and after eighteen months he reached the number-one spot! As a reward, he was given control over the other ABC affiliate in the market, the FM affiliate, which was the lowest-rated FM in the market. Six months later he had created the fastest "worst to first" turnaround for a station in Chicago history. He had created history, and he had turned a setback in Cleveland to one of the greatest comebacks in Washington and then in Chicago.

What were the steps he employed in creating his comeback?

1. Have great faith.
2. Believe in yourself and have confidence in your abilities.
3. Be willing to bet on yourself, even when others won't.
4. Constantly reaffirm your dream.
5. Focus on your destination.
6. Be willing to make tough decisions.
7. Take decisive action.
8. Remind yourself daily that you are "Blessed and Highly Favored!" When stuff happens and you are not sure of the outcome, keep repeating, "I'm Blessed and Highly Favored! I'm Blessed and Highly Favored! I'm Blessed and Highly Favored!" Believe it, and you will receive it!

JANE FLETCHER WHITE

Jane Fletcher White is an amazing woman from Houston, Texas. Jane was a music major who, two days after graduation, got her first job singing on a cruise ship headed for the Caribbean. She went on to have a very successful career singing and acting in theatres, clubs, and TV commercials. Her career took her to Houston. The first day she moved there, however, she met the love of her life, Tom White, and a year later her career took a different turn. She became his wife.

The newlyweds worked hard to save money as they wanted to buy a home and start a family. But after a year of trying, Jane was told that she might not be able to have children. She was devastated. "Why God?" she cried. "I would make such a good mother and Tom would be such a good father." Yet for some reason she suddenly felt a *peace* about her . . . a peace that God would see her through. She went on being grateful for the blessings she did have. A month later she found she was pregnant! Nine months later she went into labor and to her surprise, she delivered fifteen pounds of *babies!* That's right—boy and girl twins, Tom Jr. and Laura. Then four months later she found she was pregnant *again!* Nine months later their second daughter, Stephanie, was born. Three kids in thirteen months! Most people would be overwhelmed but Jane was not. To this day she still calls her children "God's miracle babies."

When the children were only five, six, and six, though, Jane was diagnosed with a very rare form of cancer. In fact, when the doctor told her, he said she would have to go to the hospital immediately. She was again devastated. Again came the question, "Why God?" As she was agonizing over this, a young nurse came in to take her vital signs. She tried to steer Jane away from thinking about her cancer by asking her about her family. Jane says, "As I was talking about our children I was telling her about what a wonderful father my husband was and what wonderful grandparents our parents were, and I guess my face just lit up . . . and all of a sudden, she took my hand and said, 'Mrs. White, I know you have cancer . . . but I think you are the luckiest woman I've ever met! What a family! I wish I could have had a family like yours. My parents didn't want me, so my grandma had to raise me. She didn't want me, either. If ever she didn't like something I did she would whip me and lock me in a dark closet for hours so I could think about my crime.' But then she said, 'But you know something? Now that I look back on it, it wasn't all that bad, because when I was in that closet I would think . . . *someday I'm going to get out of here and I'm going to make something of myself. But I'm going to do something where I help people, instead of hurt them*. That's why I've gone into nursing . . . and in June, I got my degree.'"

Talk about *turning a setback into a setup for a comeback,* this nurse was a perfect example of that, and Jane realized it. She says, "I realized that I had a choice on the way I was going to handle my life, just as she had. I could either sit in a corner and wait to die and be very bitter over the blow I had been dealt, or I could make the most of the days I had left, and instead of being *bitter,* try to be *better.*" Just then a feeling of peace came over me, which I can't explain. Then this phrase came into my head. *Trust in the Lord for He will see you through.*

And He has. So much so that Jane has celebrated her twenty-first year of living life to its fullest since her cancer surgery. Her mission in life now is to help others learn how to handle their situations in life, whether they be personally or professionally, so she travels the country on the speaking circuit.

The main ideas she shares with people are:

1. Put every situation you face into the *proper perspective.* Say to yourself, "In the grand scheme of things is this *really important?*" If it is, fight for it. If not, let it roll off your back. Life is too short to exhaust yourself with the trivial.
2. Never take any day, anything and, especially, *anyone* for granted. Let people know how you feel about them before it's too late.

3. Dare to take *risks*. Open as many doors as you can for yourself. It's so exciting to see what's on the other side.

4. Trust in the Lord for He will see you through.

He truly can *turn a setback into a setup for a comeback*. Jane Fletcher White is a living example.

There's No Place Like Home:
The Power of Faith, Focus, and Follow-Through!

When you change your thinking, you will see life differently and discover new treasures in old places. I found that to be true one evening while watching *The Wizard of Oz*. I had seen it dozens of times, but one night I sat with my son and watched it again. This time, I saw the story from a different perspective and discovered wonderful success secrets.

Once upon a time there was a little girl from Kansas named Dorothy. Dorothy got caught up in a storm and ended up far away from home, dazed, lost, and confused. (I realized that this is a lot like life; sometimes we all will get caught up in storms and get off track. We find ourselves in places and situations that are alien to us.) Dorothy wanted to go home, but she didn't know how. (Have you ever gotten swept off track and ended up in a strange place where you felt lost and had no idea of where or how you should proceed?) She met a lot of new people and everyone wanted to give her advice on how to solve her problem. They said, "Go to see the Wizard . . . follow the Yellow Brick Road."

She set out on her quest and along the way she came upon a scarecrow. The scarecrow was a nice fellow, but he didn't have a brain; therefore he didn't have the ability to dream. He desperately wanted a brain, so Dorothy invited him to come along with her to see the Wizard. So they set off along the Yellow Brick Road to let the Wizard make their dreams come true.

A little farther down the road they encountered a tin man, who didn't have a heart. Therefore, he didn't have the capacity to believe in his dream. Dorothy told him about the Wizard and invited him to come along so the Wizard could give him a heart. Off they went along the Yellow Brick Road. Then they came upon a cowardly lion, who didn't have the courage to live his dream (because it definitely takes courage to live your dream). He wanted to be the king of the forest, but he was afraid. They realized he needed courage to be the king of the forest. They invited him to go along to see the Wizard.

Along the way they encountered obstacles and challenges and life-threatening situations, but they kept going because they felt they needed the Wizard to make them complete. Finally, after many tests and trials they got to see the Wizard, and found out he was a fake, a phony, a pretender. He wasn't able to help them. In fact, he was still trying to figure out how to get his own life together.

They were devastated. All their hard work was in vain. They had done so much to get to the Wizard, just to find that he was not able to help them get back home. As they cried over their problems, they got a visit from Glinda, the Good Witch. She looked at them with pity and said, "You didn't need the Wizard to go back home. You had it within you all the time. All you had to do was to believe, and click your heels together three times."

At that moment I thought of the wonderful quote from Emerson that states: "That which is before and that which is behind you can never compare with that which is within you!" In my mind's eye I could see the group standing there looking in amazement as Glinda uttered those words, "It was within you all the time." In my mind, I saw Glinda then giving them the formula for turning their challenges into opportunities. The formula for turning their problems into possibilities and turning their setbacks into setups for comebacks was with them all along. I closed my eyes and visualized her saying, "Just believe and click your heels three times, once for faith, once for focus, and once for follow-through. And if you sincerely want it badly enough, you will go home." Dorothy clicked three times, and she went home!

Friends, everything you need to make your dreams come true is already within you, just click your heels together three times. Click once for *faith,* which the Bible says is the ability "to call forth things that be not, as though they are! Or as Les Brown says, "Faith is the willingness to jump . . . and know that the net will appear!" Occasionally we all get caught up in storms and lose our way home. Take time to pray and seek guidance, and work on building your faith because it's like a muscle, the more you use it the stronger it gets. As you strengthen your faith, you will be able to stand in the middle of the storms and not give up. Faith gives us the ability to believe that our dreams are possible.

In the Broadway adaptation of *The Wizard of Oz,* which was entitled, *The Wiz,* Glinda sang a song called "If You Believe," right before showing them how to click their heels three times. She said if you believe within your heart you can go home. You must believe if you want to turn your setbacks into comebacks. You must believe that you can and believe that you will. Develop the belief that it is impossible for you to fail. Then act on that belief. You will not fail. You will have setbacks, but you will no longer see them as failures but will see them as setups for incredible comebacks.

Next you will click for *focus.* Focus on the possibilities, not on the problems. Focus on the positive perspective, not the negative perspective. Focus on your goals, not on your obstacles. Focus your energies on the major issues at hand and not on all the minor nuisances that will try to steal your time and energy. Focus on the options available to you. The person who is able to harness and focus their energies creates the fires of life, not those whose energies are fractured and disjointed. Click for focus.

The third click is for *follow-through,* because you must take action if you want to turn your setbacks into comebacks. When you believe that you will find a way and then act on those beliefs with the expectation that your actions will reap positive results, you will start to fly. Unfortunately, many people have faith but no follow-through. God gives the bird its food, but He does not throw it into their nest. It takes faith and action, because faith without works is dead. Have faith, stay focused, and follow-through: take action.

James Carter and Ramon Williamson have written a book called *22 Uncommon Ways to Success,* in which one of the chapters says it wonderfully: "Walk by faith . . . but run when you can!" Friends, you need faith to turn a setback into a setup for a comeback, but it takes action. Faith and action are a powerful team. Don't leave home without them! Just click your heels three times, with faith, focus, and follow-through, and remember . . . there's no place like home, there's no place like home, there's no place like home!

> *Faith is to believe what we do not see and the reward of faith is to see what we believe.*
>
> —Saint Augustine

Step Ten: Teaching Points:

1. Determine where is your faith? Is it in God or in the circumstances?
2. What others mean for bad, God means for good. Just have faith.

3. Live your faith, not your fears.
4. FEAR versus FAITH = false evidence appearing real versus finding answers in the heart.
5. God is not a one-idea God.
6. Stay "Blessed and Highly Favored." Speak it and live it!
7. Take count of your blessings, not your problems.
8. Be willing to bet on yourself even when others won't.
9. Faith is stepping out on nothing and believing you will land on something.
10. Click your heels three times, once for faith, then for focus, then for follow-through. Find the power deep inside of you and you will find your way home.

Step Eleven

Say, "Yes!": Make a Commitment
to Your Commitment!
Affirm to Win, Refuse to Lose,
and Never Give Up!

*It's not whether you get knocked down. It's whether you
get up again.*

—Vince Lombardi

*The measure of a man is the way he bears up under misfortune. I may be wounded, but I am not slain. I shall lay
me down and bleed awhile, but I will rise and fight again!*

—Plutarch

◇ ◇ ◇Okay folks, this is it, "Straight, no chaser" (as they used
to say in the nightclubs where I sang). When all is said and
done (and much more is said than done), you must never stop
trying! To turn a setback into a comeback you must be committed and never give up. It is not an option. It is absolutely
mandatory. You must never give up!

You must make a commitment to keep going. Then make a
commitment to your commitment. Commitment is critical to
turning a setback into a setup for a comeback. That is when
you realize the power that is within you. Commitment is the
act of emotionally compelling yourself to a position where you
refuse to stop until you achieve your goal. It is a willingness to

do everything you can, everything you know, and everything you can think of to reach your goal. And when you commit yourself you will discover you have power you didn't even know you had. It takes commitment, serious commitment.

The Power of Commitment

In life you are either just interested in a relationship or committed to a relationship. You are either just interested in completing your studies or committed to completing your studies. You are either just interested in starting your own business, following your dream or committed to it. You are either just interested in improving your health, income, or lifestyle or you are committed to it. You are either just interested in reducing the stress and mess in your life or you are committed to it. Once you make up your mind, the main thing is to keep The Main Thing . . . The Main Thing. Stay focused and committed and you will see results . . . not regrets.

—Jewel Diamond Taylor, Author and Speaker

Along with commitment you also need courage, because life will knock you down and try to knock you out. It takes courage to get back up and fight. Life will try to scare you. But you must have courage and get back up on your feet and keep fighting! You have had a setback, you've been knocked to the canvas, and you've decided to get back in the ring. What's next? Next you've got to fight and fight with all your might. Fight with an expectation that you will win, because your expectations directly impact your results.

In his book, *Trump: The Art of the Comeback,* Donald Trump wrote:

In order to comeback you must be willing to fight, and fight hard. And you must expect to win. You will need confidence, determination, and persistence. And you must take adversity and make it an asset. This means finding creative ways to make the best of both good and bad situations. Finally, in order to comeback you have got to have a champion's heart. Talent is not enough, hard work is not enough, you have got to have a champion's heart and then go out and get it done.

Friends, the race does not go to the swift or to the strong but to the one who endures until the end! Expect to win, refuse to lose, and no matter what happens, never give up!

> *Decide to be unstoppable. You may stumble, and you may fall, but you must not stop!*
>
> —Willie Jolley

I heard a story about a lady who was the leading salesperson in her company. She was scheduled to get the Number-One Salesperson Award at the company's annual banquet. This lady was a real success story. She had risen above numerous obstacles to achieve her goals and was an inspiration to all of her coworkers.

On the night of the banquet, everyone was dressed in their best clothes and anxiously awaiting the moment when the Number-One Salesperson Award would be announced. When the lady's name was called, everyone in the room broke into a tremendous applause because she had overcome so much to achieve this honor. As she ran up the steps to accept her award and make her acceptance speech, she tripped on the top step, fell, and slammed facedown onto the stage floor.

The room immediately became eerily silent. No one knew

what to do or say because it was such an embarrassing incident. After lying there for a moment, she jumped up, ran to the podium, took the award in her hands, and said, "Folks, many of you have asked what I did to win this award. Well, you just witnessed it. See, I fall down a lot . . . but I keep getting back up! And that is why I am getting this award tonight, because I just keep getting back up!"

One evening after a speech I sat in a hotel room and started flipping the channels. I came across a video channel and heard a song that mesmerized me. The singer seemed to be hollering the lyrics, but the music was very catchy. I listened for a minute and found that there was something special about this song. The singer was screaming, "I get knocked down, but I get up again; you're never gonna keep me down" and he repeated the lyrics over and over again.

I soon realized that this wasn't just a regular everyday rock song, but it was a "pick yourself up from the floor" song. What a powerful message! It had such an infectious beat and chant that I left the hotel that day saying, "I get knocked down, but I get up again, 'cause you're never gonna keep me down!" I don't know if the style of music is your cup of tea, but I do believe that the words and the message apply to us all. Yes, life sometimes knocks us down, but we must make a commitment to get up again; a commitment that nothing is ever going to keep us down! You might get knocked down many times, but resolve that nothing, no-thing, will ever keep you down. Get back up and never give up!

One of the keys to turning your setbacks into a comeback is to identify your reasons for coming back. They will compel you to keep getting up. As Nietzsche said, "If you know the WHY, you can withstand any HOW!" Everett Hall is an excellent example of someone who has focused on his reasons. And those reasons have led to incredible results!

Everett Hall is a name that is becoming synonymous with

high fashion around the world. He is one of the top designers for the NBA sports stars (and he has even made a few speakers look good, including one from Washington, D.C.). I stopped by Everett's store in Washington, D.C. and asked him about setbacks. He said, "Do you want the ones today or yesterday?" In other words, he made it clear that setbacks are part of his daily routine. As we talked, he shared his perspective on setbacks and how to turn them into setups for comebacks.

Everett said that he has had so many setbacks that it is hard to remember them all! Yet his perspective about setbacks is consistent with all the other people I interviewed. They view setbacks as growth experiences disguised as setbacks. Everett said, "You know the old saying is true, a problem is nothing but an opportunity in work clothes. And if your reasons are strong enough, they will lead to results!" Focus on the *why*. Why are you doing this? Why do you want to reach this goal? Why are you willing to do what is uncomfortable? Why are you willing to keep going in spite of the challenges? If the reasons are strong enough, you will become unstoppable!

I share with my audiences how I became friends with Everett Hall. His store is next to a very popular restaurant in Washington. I was going to dinner with my wife and we were a bit early, so we decided to walk around the mall. We stopped by Everett's store. He mentioned he had some of my books and tapes and thanked me for them. He explained how they had been influential in his reaching some of his goals. He asked if we had a few minutes and I said, "Yes." He took us down to the garage and led us to his latest "goal." He showed us his new, black Rolls-Royce Convertible! I said, "You got that from reading my books and listening to my tapes?! I'm going to go re-read my books and listen to my tapes too!" We laughed, but in reality it was not just my tapes, but also Les Brown tapes, Zig Ziglar tapes, Jim Rhone tapes, Brian Tracy tapes, and many more in the back of his car. Everett realized that self-development is a major part of success. It is your input that determines your output.

I asked Everett what was the defining moment that took him from being a young guy making clothes in Springfield, Ohio, to becoming one of America's hottest designers, and the designer of choice for many of the rich and famous. He looked up and, without a minute's hesitation, said, "The day my dad died! That was the defining moment!"

Everett explained that when he was growing up his father loved clothes. He taught his sons to appreciate clothes and how to respect and take care of the clothes that they had. His dad was an assembly line worker and couldn't afford an expensive wardrobe so he encouraged his sons to learn to make their own! Everett excelled in the process. Everett's first creation was a very stylish pair of pants. The pockets didn't work and one leg was shorter than the other, but his brothers thought they were cool. They asked him to make them a pair. Soon everyone in the school wanted a pair. In his first year, he made over three hundred items.

Everett remembered one time he was making some clothes and ran out of fabric and told his dad that he really needed the fabric to finish the suit. His father did not have a car at that time, so he walked a number of miles to the store to purchase the fabric while Everett continued to sew.

While we were talking, Everett's brother Eric came in the room and shared a story that both agreed was another pivotal time in their lives. They were in undergraduate school and didn't have enough money to go back for the new semester. They had tapped all of their resources. Their father came home from a long night at work, and the boys told him of their problem. He took out his vacation check, which he had been saving for months, went to the bank and cashed it. He took out fifty dollars for himself and gave the boys the rest. Both brothers looked at each other and said, "That was commitment!"

Their father worked hard to make sure that his sons had whatever they needed to succeed. Unfortunately, he didn't get to personally see it. He died at the age of forty-five. When his father died Everett made a promise that he would always give his best. He would not let anything keep him from being the best. He made a commitment to excellence. Work on self, make a commitment to excellence, and then make a commitment to your commitment! And when you get knocked down, always remember your *why,* which is your reason for getting back up.

Everett detailed his principles for success and said if you understand the principles and apply the principles, you can consistently turn your setbacks into comebacks. Here are his principles:

1. When you have a setback you must make a conscious decision to view it, not as a problem, but rather as a learning opportunity.
2. You must decide what you're going to do about it: Are you going to give up, or are you going to get up and fight?
3. You must focus on your goal. What is it you are trying to achieve?
4. You must employ faith and know that if God is with you, then He's greater than the whole world against you.
5. You must take action and keep taking action until you reach your goal, no matter what life throws at you.
6. You must work on yourself and make a commitment to excellence. Then make a commitment to the commitment.

7. Remember, your input determines your output.
8. Have a reason why, so you can always remember your reasons for getting up every time you are knocked down.

Develop a Steel Will, and Will Yourself to Win!

Just as you develop muscles by exercising them, you also develop a steel will by exercising it. Just refuse to give up and give in to the setbacks. If you make up your mind that you are going to reach your goal, no matter what, you usually will. Those who turn back are those who are not really committed. They might say they are committed, but they really aren't. A friend, Bill Cates, the Referral Coach says, "Freedom is when you have made a decision to win and have cut off all of your options." He says it is liberating when you commit yourself and make up your mind that you will do or die, sink or swim. That is when you are energized and determined to achieve your goal or else.

Still Kicking! The Ageless Story of Bill Clark

Bill Clark is another great example of commitment and the power of having *reasons* to get back up after being knocked down. Bill Clark worked for the park service and was working long hours and spending few hours at home with his children. He decided to take martial arts lessons with his son, so they could have more quality time together. Bill was in his forties and was not in great shape, but he felt that he could at least get some exercise. They started the classes and Bill quickly realized he not only enjoyed martial arts but was also very good at it. He quickly surpassed all the younger students and soon became a star student. He started moving toward his black belt. Martial arts became his passion, and he would work on it at every available moment.

Finally Bill was up for his black belt. He had passed the other exercises and had even broken bricks. He had only one last test to go through, which was breaking two boards with a flying sidekick. While in the air, he realized he had jumped too far and might hurt his partner who was holding the boards. So he turned his body to avoid injuring his partner and landed wrong and his leg snapped. He broke his leg in seven places and was rushed to the hospital. The doctors said it was one of the worst breaks they had ever seen. According to the doctors, it was comparable to a major motorcycle collision. They predicted about six months out of work and six to eight months before he would be able to walk. They also told him he would never be able to do martial arts again. Bill decided that the doctors were mistaken! He had found something that he loved and it had become a family activity. He was determined he was going to turn this setback into a comeback.

Bill went to work on his comeback immediately after getting home from the hospital. He started doing exercises from his bed, for he was determined that he was going to prove the doctors wrong. In four weeks he was back at work on crutches. In seven weeks he was walking with only a cane. Amazingly, he was back to instructing classes with the kids in eight weeks, while still in a cast! At the twelve-week mark, he was back working out at the martial arts studio on his upper body exercises and working with his "good" leg. In seven months he laughed at the doctors and was back kicking and jumping again and breaking boards. Bill went on to get his black belt and has since gotten a number of higher-level belts.

What were the steps that Bill took to make this impossible dream become possible? The steps were:

1. A positive attitude, a positive perspective, and positive perseverance. He realized that it is the mental strength that overcomes physical limitations.
2. He saw it not as a problem, but rather as a learning experience.
3. When others said it was the end of his martial arts career, he saw it as a new beginning.
4. Where others saw it as a BIG DEAL, he saw it as a small deal. Just a bump in the road!
5. Bill realized "stuff" happens. To win in life you must be willing to find what you want and not be discouraged. Decide! Have a positive mental attitude and then do it!

Bill Clark is a living example of someone who turned a setback into a setup for a comeback. He did it with a positive mental attitude. After coming back and earning his next level belt, he was given a special award of merit from the Korean Martial Arts Research Association for his inspirational comeback. The award reads: "Awarded to Bill Clark for courage, strength, perseverance, and your indomitable spirit and confidence of certain victory. We applaud you for your accomplishments and the outstanding model you have given to your classmates, as well as your instructions. You have taught us all about overcoming obstacles, and you have shown us what it really takes to be a winner!"

One of the keys to commitment is the importance of working on self and developing leadership qualities. Leaders are like diamonds, they are not born; they are developed. Commitment helps us realize that success is a do-it-yourself project . . . it is ultimately up to you!

Just like the biblical story of Job, whose friends criticized and rejected him when the tough times came, there is a story about a man named Roger Johnson. He learned about how tough times impact friendships. Roger Johnson built a successful manufacturing company and employed his friends to work for him. Then the tough times came, and his friends left one by one. Eventually everyone left, but he didn't give up. He fought for his company and he fought for his dream. He kept fighting and he turned the company around and staged an incredible comeback. He learned that success is ultimately your own responsibility, because you can be assured that the only person who is guaranteed never to leave you is YOU!

The Power of Self-Development

When you have a setback, sometimes you must step back and look at yourself and ask, "What do I need to do to ensure that this doesn't happen again?" When I was a youngster I remember reading the comics about the ninety-pound weakling who got sand kicked in his face by the bully. The bully even took his girlfriend. The ninety-pound weakling decided he could not control what happened to him, but he could control what he did about it. He started eating healthy foods and going to the gym and working out. He started lifting weights and he got bigger and bigger, and stronger and stronger. Not only did more girls find him attractive, but the bully decided to leave him alone. I learned a lesson from that cartoon. In order to become all you can be, you must constantly work on yourself and become a leader of one. Before you can lead many, you must be able to lead one—yourself!

Leaders of One!
In order to effectively live your dreams you must become a leader of one! If not, life will always lead you and you will always be blown by the winds of change. I say you can't control which way the wind is going to blow, but you can use the wind to go where you want to go. If you look at sailboats on

the river, you will see that the wind may be blowing to the south and there will be some boats that will be going with the flow, going south. Yet if you look, there will also be some boats that will be going north and others that will be going east to west. The wind might be blowing to the south but that does not mean you have to go with the flow or where the wind wants you to go; you can use the wind to go where you want to go. It might not be easy, but it can be done . . . and if it can be done, it must be done! In order to effectively navigate the winds of change you must become a leader of one.

We all have setbacks but we must be honest and wise enough to look objectively at ourselves and see if we are the cause of some of our problems. In order to grow we must look at ourselves and learn from our mistakes. The people who consistently win are the people who are willing to look at themselves and learn from their mistakes. Those people who don't learn from their mistakes are destined to repeat them and destined to live below their potential. Leaders learn, leaders take responsibility, and leaders understand that they must not just "go through situations" but must more importantly "grow through them." This is a verse that was adapted by my friend, Rev. Lamar McClain, author of the book *God of the Valley:*

> *He who Knows Not, and Knows Not that he Knows Not,*
> *but thinks he Knows, is a fool . . . shun him!*
> *He who Knows Not, and Knows that he Knows Not,*
> *is a child . . . teach him!*
> *He who Knows, but uses not what he Knows,*
> *is asleep . . . wake him!*
> *Oh, but he who Knows, and Knows that he Knows,*
> *and uses what he Knows is a leader . . . follow him!*
>
> —Author Unknown

I ask you, with these four levels of knowing, which level are you?

Four Levels of Consciousness

Now, let's focus on the four levels of consciousness that affect our performance in life. First, there is the level of *unconscious incompetence*, which means to be unable to properly perform a task, and not realize that you are unable to perform the task. Second is the level of *conscious incompetence*, which means to be unable to perform a task but you are aware of your inability to perform that task.

The third level of consciousness is *conscious competence*, which means to know that you are able to perform a task and to think about it as you perform it.

Finally, the fourth level is *unconscious competence*, which means that you are not only able to perform the task but it is so ingrained, so much a part of you, that you do not even have to think about it: You just do it! This was best seen in the mastery of Michael Jordan on a basketball court, when he would create an amazing shot while actually flying through the air. He didn't even think about it . . . he just did it! We should all work toward this level of competence in our performance. Then we too will be able to do incredible things!

Commitment, persistence, and dogged determination are keys in turning your setbacks into comebacks. You must simply keep moving toward your goal. As A. L. Williams says, "All you can do is all you can do, and all you can do is enough. Just make sure that all you can do is absolutely all that you can do!

Step Eleven: Teaching Points:

1. Make a commitment. Then make a commitment to your commitment.
2. It is not whether you get knocked down; it is whether you get up again.

3. Expect to win, refuse to lose, and never give up.
4. Set priorities and keep the main thing the main thing.
5. Develop a strong will to win.
6. No matter how many times you fail, keep getting back up.
7. If you know the why, you can withstand any how. Focus on the why.
8. You are the only one who will never leave you, so learn to love you.
9. Before you can lead many, you must be able to lead one.
10. There's no substitute for excellence, so make excellence a priority.

Step Twelve

It's All Good: Be Thankful!
Have an Attitude of Gratitude!

*All things work together for the good for those who love the
Lord and are called according to His purposes!*
—Romans 8:28

◇ ◇ ◇ Charles Spurgeon, the noted English clergyman, noticed that the weather vane on the roof of a farm building bore
the phrase "God is Love" and was troubled. "Do you think
God's love is as changeable as that weather vane?" he asked
the farmer. "You miss the point, good sir," replied the farmer.
"It's on the weather vane because no matter which way the
wind is blowing, God is still love." No matter which way the
wind blows, it's all good, because in time all things really do
work together for the good.

In order to completely turn a setback into a setup for a
comeback you must come to the conclusion that it is all good.
It really is all good! Over the last few years young people
across America have established a new discourse. It goes
something like this:

"How're you doing?"

"Cool!"

"What's happening?"

"It's all good!"

"Yeah, it's all good!"

I do not know if they truly understand the power of that

statement, but I am glad they are saying it. And therefore they are speaking it into being. No matter what happens in life, it's all good! It's a wonderful way to reply to life; just know it's all good! I shared a story in my first book that has gotten such a positive response that I must share it in this book. I think this so wonderfully illustrates that everything is "all good" because truly all things really do work together for the good!

All Things Work Together for Good . . .

Once upon a time there was a wise Chinese father in a small community. This wise father was held in high esteem, not so much because of his wisdom, but because of his two possessions: a strong son and a horse. One day the horse broke through the fence and ran away. All the neighbors came around and said, "What bad luck!" and the wise father replied, "Why do you call it bad luck?" A few days later the horse came back with ten other horses, and all the neighbors said, "What good luck!" and the wise father responded, "Why do you call it good luck?" A few days later his strong son went out to the corral to break in one of the new horses, and he was thrown off and broke his hip. All the neighbors came over and said, "What bad luck!" and the wise father responded, "Why do you call it bad luck?"

About a week later the evil warlord came through the town and gathered all of the strong, able-bodied young men and took them off to war. The only one he did not take was the boy with the broken hip. All the young men were killed in battle, and when the news reached the community, the neighbors rushed to the father and said, "What good luck!" The father said, "Luck? No! It is not luck! All things work together for the good, for those who love the Lord!"

There may be times when things really look tough and

when things do not go as you planned. But if you look hard enough and have faith, you will see that with every blessing there is a burden, and with every burden, there is a blessing. Every dark cloud has a silver lining, if you are willing to look for it and learn from it.

The Power of Vision, Decision, Action, Desire, and Faith!

Sometimes in life we have teeth-rattling experiences and we run to God because our world is shaking, only to find out that it is God who is doing the shaking.

—Author Unknown

Sometimes God has to get our attention and uses challenging experiences to do so. Yet these experiences can change our lives. Not long after I had been fired from my nightclub job and had started working with the school system, I got a letter from the Gospel Music Association. The letter stated that someone had heard me sing and recommended me to perform for their Annual New Artist Showcase. Every major record company would be there, and there would be record contracts given on the spot. WOW! That was it. I was going to be a star!

I said to myself, I am going to get a record contract; I'm going to be famous! I went to Nashville, Tennessee, with quite a swagger. I was planning to put on a show like those folks had never seen before. I walked off that plane like I was a star, I had my black shades on and my coat draped over my shoulders. I got to the hotel and told the people at the registration desk, with a definite arrogance, "Have no fear, I am here!" I walked into the ballroom that night with a serious attitude. I was a "badd dude." I was cocky and arrogant. I got up on that stage that night, and I was "badd." I walked in front of that microphone, and I was "badd." I started to sing, and I was "BAD, REAL BAD, TERRIBLY BAD!!!"

Oh, the notes were right. The tune was right. The music was technically right. But the motive was wrong! I had gone up on that stage to impress the audience, when I should have gone on that stage to inspire the audience! It was the most humiliating night of my life! I was accustomed to audiences giving me a standing ovation after my performances. This night they didn't even clap. As I walked through the audience, they just turned and looked away. I was devastated! I went back to my little hotel room and I cried. I cried and I cried and finally, in complete despair, I screamed, "What Do You Want?" And the answer came as clear as a bell, "Inspire others! Do not try to impress them, but rather inspire them. If you inspire, you will not have to be concerned about the impression; it will take care of itself. Inspire people!"

It was at that moment that my life changed. It was a moment of adversity and pain; yet it was also a moment of definition. The spirit was so strong. Then the voice told me to take out a piece of paper and start writing. The voice said, "Write the word *InspirTainment Plus,* which means inspiration and entertainment." I said, "Wow, that's a great name; I like it!" Then the voice said, "You're going to speak to millions of people; write it down!" I said, "I'm not a speaker. I just give those little speeches for the kids; but I'm really not a speaker, I'm a singer." He said, "Write it down!"

Next the voice said, "You're going to write books. Write it down!" "But I am not a writer." He said, "Write it down!" I finally figured out I had better write it down. So I wrote it down. He said, "You're going to do television and radio. Write it down." "But, God, I have no experience in television and radio, but I'm going to write it down." Then He said, "Go home and quit your job!" I said, "What? What was that? Hello? Have you checked out my bank account recently? I have two hundred dollars to my name." He said, "Go home and quit your job. Just Trust Me!"

I went home and got off the plane and saw my wife. I walked over to her and showed her my vision sheet and said, "I'm going to quit my job!" (Thank God I have a wonderful wife. Even though she might have thought I was crazy, she never questioned me or doubted me.) I walked into the office the next day and announced that I was going to leave my job and become a full-time speaker. They all looked at me like I was crazy. "You're going to leave your 'good government job' to become a speaker? You're going to starve." "Maybe, but I have faith that God will do what He said He'd do, and I was willing to bet my future on it." I walked out that day and they questioned my sanity. They said I wouldn't make it. They said that I would starve to death. They said I was a fool for leaving my job to follow a dream.

Well, in the few years since I left that job, I have spoken to over a million people in America and abroad. I have a syndicated radio and television show. I have written bestselling books, and I have recorded bestselling albums. I have had the opportunity to appear on stage with some of the greatest speakers and entertainers in the world. And it all started by failing. Having a setback.

From that setback I learned about the power of a vision, the power of decision, the power of action, and the power of desire! I learned that a setback is really nothing but a setup for a comeback! Most importantly, I learned about the power of faith and how to walk by faith. God got my attention and turned my life around by using a setback. He is not a respecter of persons. He will do for others what He has done for one. But it takes Vision, Decision, Action, Desire, and Faith!

Pray for vision. Then make the tough decisions. Take massive action. Develop a tremendous desire to achieve your goals. And have faith. Have faith that God wants you to succeed, but you must work and truly believe that you can.

Focus on the Solution, Not on the Problem!

When you have a setback you must focus your energies. Unfortunately, most people focus on the problem and not on the solution. They take their eyes off the goal and focus on the challenges all around the goal. They spend all of their time worrying about the problem and very little time thinking about the solution. If you are going to think about and dwell on what might happen, why not think about the good things that can happen, the positive things that can happen?

Worry does not solve problems. It usually adds to them. Worrying is a misuse of the imagination. Most people worry themselves into bad health, which creates more problems and more worries. Medical experts agree that most disease is not so much what you eat, but rather what is eating you. Worrying never solves problems. Do not focus your energies on the problem, because the problem is already here. Focus on creating solutions and then acting on the solutions. The solution is waiting to be born, waiting to be discovered, waiting to be uncovered, but you must bring it to life. Act and unleash the wonderful answers that will make the problem a thing of the past and make the solution a thing of the present.

In life, we will have challenges. We will have problems. We will have setbacks. Just keep in mind that there is no use in crying when it's raining, and there is no use in worrying about the problems. Focus your energy on the solution and not on the problem, and remember that a setback is nothing but a setup for a comeback!

Be Thankful! Have an Attitude of Gratitude

Two men are walking down a country road and one asks the other, "How are you doing?" The first farmer says, "The ground is hard, the cows are old, the milk isn't as sweet as it used to be. Everything is just terrible. Life stinks! How are you doing?"

The second farmer replied, "Well, the ground is hard over here too, but I am thankful because I remember when I didn't have any ground. And this hard ground is much better than no ground at all. My cows aren't as young as they used to be either, but they are still making milk, and the milk is still selling. I don't have a lot but I do have my health, and I'm still able to get up every day and go out and do what I love. I am very thankful. I thank God for everything!"

As time went by the farmer who was negative continued to complain about life and continued to find all the negative aspects of life he could find. Eventually he complained and worried himself into an early grave. The farmer who was positive continued to work hard and continued to enjoy life. Most of all he continued to be thankful and lived to a ripe old age. He had a good, positive reason to get up every morning. See, as praises and gratitude go up, blessings and wonders come down. Look at the positive and find that there is always something to be thankful about if you are willing to look for it! Always keep an attitude of gratitude and realize that life really is a wonderful thing. Setbacks happen to us all, but those who are optimistic are willing to go forward with a confidence that no matter what happens, it will all work for the good. The results will ultimately be in your favor. But it's your choice!

This book is about choice. You have a choice in life. You might not be able to choose what happens to you, but you can control what happens in you. And you can control what you do about what happens to you. It's about choice. Choose to be happy. Choose to keep going, even when times are tough. Choose to have a positive attitude. Choose to be optimistic; expect good things to result from your actions. Choose to work on yourself. Make motivation and inspiration a part of your daily routine. Choose to have faith, because every day above ground is a good day.

Over the years I have sung an old hymn called "We'll Understand It Better, By and By!" I have sung it hundreds of times, but it was not until recently that I truly understood it. The lyrics are:

We are often tossed and driven on the restless sea of time
Somber skies and howling tempests oft succeed a bright sunshine
In that land of perfect day, when the mists have rolled away
We will understand it better by and by

Temptations, hidden snares often take us unawares
And our hearts are made to bleed for many a thoughtless word or deed
And we wonder why the test when we try to do our best
But we'll understand it better by and by

By and by when the morning comes
When all the saints of God are gathered home
We'll tell the story of how we've overcome
For we'll understand it better by and by.

The lyrics state that even though we will all go through challenging times, do not despair, have faith and hold on. For we will understand it better by and by. I look back now and realize that I did not understand it when I was fired from my singing job. I did not understand it when I bombed on the stage at the Gospel Music Association in Nashville, Tennessee. They were all setbacks. I did not understand why then, but in time I understood it much better.

If I had not been fired from my singing job and replaced by a karaoke machine, I would not have taken a job with the school system. If I had not taken a job with the school system, I probably would not have started speaking. If I had never started speaking, I would have never joined the National Speakers Association. If I had not joined the National Speakers Association, I would not have been invited to speak at the 1994 National Speakers Association Convention. If I had not been invited to speak at that convention, I would not have met book publicist, Rick Frishman. If Rick Frishman had not heard me speak, then he would have not have referred me to literary agent, Jeff Herman. If I had never been referred to Jeff Herman, he would never have been able to negotiate a book deal with St. Martin's Press. And if there were no book deal, *you* would not be reading this book!

And it all started with a setback, a setback of being fired from a singing job and being replaced by a karaoke machine! Which led to another setback in Nashville, where I was embarrassed and humiliated, yet I was able to learn a valuable lesson about the power of inspiration. That led to another setback on my job with the school system, where I had to make a decision of whether to do what was necessary or do what was comfortable. I decided to quit and walk by faith. From there I started speaking and created a one-minute radio show that created a book of one-minute motivational messages. And now there is a book about turning setbacks into comebacks. And this all started with a setback! Oh, yes, I do finally understand that a setback is nothing but a setup for a comeback!

I didn't understand it then, but I understand it now. If I just have faith, and keep going and keep the vision clearly in sight, then my setbacks will become stepping stones to my dreams. I have found it to be true; a setback really is nothing but a setup for a comeback! No matter what happens . . . it's all good!

The Burning Hut!

The only survivor of a shipwreck washed up on a small, uninhabited island. He prayed feverishly for God to rescue him, and every day he scanned the horizon for help, but none seemed forthcoming. Exhausted, he eventually managed to build a little hut out of driftwood to protect him from the elements and to store his few possessions.

But then one day while scavenging for food, he saw a flash of lightning. He arrived home to find his little hut in flames, with the dark smoke rolling up to the sky. The worst had happened; everything was lost. He was stung with grief and anger. "God, how could you do this to me?" he cried. Yet somewhere in his pain he found the strength to say, "I must continue to have faith; I must continue to have faith." Early the next day he was awakened by the sound of a ship that was approaching the island. It had come to rescue him. "How did you know I was here?" asked the weary man of his rescuers. "It was your smoke signal," they replied.

Friends, it is easy to get discouraged when things are going bad. But we shouldn't lose heart, because God is at work in our lives, even in the midst of the challenges. God's delay is not God's denial. Remember, the next time your little hut is burning to the ground—it just may be a smoke signal that turns your life around and brings help your way. Your world is shaking and you run to God . . . only to find out that it is God who is doing the shaking. Well, God's in the shaking, God's in the breaking, but always remember, God's in the making!

Have faith, believe in your dreams, take action, and always remember that setbacks are a part of life. Setbacks are going to happen, whether you like them or not. So get a new perspective! Realize it only takes a minute to change your life and turn it around. The minute you make a decision, take action, move toward your vision, and do so with great desire, you will change your life. You will start turning your setbacks into comebacks. Remember, it takes Vision, Decision, Action, and Desire. If you can do this, you too will be able to say, in the midst of a setback, "Oh, what a wonderful minute . . . A setback is nothing but a setup for a comeback, and I'm coming back!" Friends, do it *now!* It is within your grasp. And remember, it only takes a minute to change your life, so make every minute count! And you'll find that *all* your setbacks are nothing but setups for comebacks! God bless!

Step Twelve: Teaching Points

1. No matter what happens, it's all good!
2. All things work together for the good.
3. Ain't no use in crying when it's raining; focus on the solution not the problem.
4. Have an attitude of gratitude.
5. Sometimes it's God who is doing the shaking as well as the making.
6. Worry never solves any problem, but action does.
7. Choose to Win! Choose to be healthy, wealthy, wise, happy, and thankful.
8. Your burning hut may be a smoke signal for greater success.
9. Vision, Decision, Action, and Desire are a powerful team. Don't leave home without them!
10. It only takes a minute to make a comeback. The minute you decide and take action, you're on your way!

Epilogue

❖ ❖ ❖ This book has been a labor of love. It has been challenging and difficult. I have had a number of setbacks in the process. I have had to write, rewrite, then rewrite again. I have had major computer problems and time crunches. I have had heartaches because I was unable to get on paper what I had in my heart, yet I persisted and I refused to give up. And I have grown because of it. I am confident that the person I am now, at the end, is a much different person from the person I was at the beginning of this process.

I pray that I have reached my objectives. My first objective was to inspire you. I hope this book has been able to "breathe anew" and inspire you with new ideas and insights into how to view setbacks and problems in your life. I hope that you have been motivated as well as inspired. Therefore you will not only be moved in a motivational sense, with your mind, but you will also be inspired to act with your heart.

My second objective was to give you information. Motivation and inspiration without information is incomplete. I hope you have been given good "How to's," some "Aha's," and "Teaching Points" that will illuminate effective TIPS (techniques, ideas, principles, and strategies) for success.

My third objective was to share my philosophy and some of my theological perspectives in a way that was simple yet enlightening. I wanted to make it simple enough that a child could read it and understand it, yet informative and compelling enough that a college scholar could read and enjoy it. It was difficult but I have tried to make it a book that would be of help to a great number of people.

Finally, I desperately wanted to share my faith and my heart, not just my words. I am so thankful for what God has done in my life, and just as if I would share with friends a great restaurant or a great movie, I wanted to share the joy and fulfillment I have received as a result of making a commitment to my faith. If you have finished this book and still have no one to call on, no one to pray to, no one whom you can feel comfortable calling your God, then let me make a recommendation. This is someone who has helped me and has shown me that a setback is nothing but a setup for a comeback.

He was a young man who died in his early thirties after a brief public career had brought him fame in his time and territory. The tragic element of his life story is that after a stunning success he was falsely accused of a crime that resulted in his imprisonment, trial, and execution. The death penalty was carried out. The end of his life was utter disgrace, humiliation, and shame. I would weep as I think of the whole sad, sordid spectacle of this social injustice, except that his name was eventually vindicated. He came back and his comeback was stunning and spectacular. His honor was restored and elevated. His name today is the most respected and renowned name in the world. Today, we even count the years by Him, the time before his death and the time after his death. His name is Jesus and He is my friend and inspiration. I know if you will just call . . . He will answer! Just try Him. I am sure you will like Him. (Adapted from Dr. Robert Schuller.)

Thanks for reading and sharing the thoughts of my heart. I

pray that you will share this information with others, who will share it with others, and the process will continue. And people will see, in massive numbers, that a "bend in the road is not the end of the road!" Go forth and live your dreams, with power, passion, and purpose. Remember, you were born for a reason and with a mission and you must live it!

Always stay "Blessed and Highly Favored," even in the midst of the challenges. I leave you with this quote by Nelson Mandela: "The greatest power in life is not never falling, but in rising every time you fall." Keep rising! Go forth and remember that "a Setback Is Nothing but a Setup for a Comeback!"

Remember:

> *You have Only Just A Minute,*
> *Only sixty seconds in it*
> *Forced upon You, can't refuse it,*
> *Didn't seek it, Didn't choose it*
> *But it's up to You to use it,*
> *You must suffer if You lose it*
> *Give account if You abuse it,*
> *Just a tiny little minute, but an Eternity is in it!*

For more information on
Willie Jolley and his
motivational programs,
products, and service,
contact:
http://www.williejolley.com
or call 1-800-487-8899 or
The Willie Jolley Motivational Hotline
1-888-2MOTIV8
(1-888-266-8488)

About the Author

◇◇◇ Willie Jolley is America's leading motivational speaker/singer combination! He is an award-winning speaker, singer, bestselling author, and media personality. He is the creator of "InspirTainment Plus" and the president of the Jolley Leadership Training and Development Institute. The JLTD Institute works with organizations that want to rapidly accelerate growth and create top performers. Mr. Jolley speaks worldwide for corporations, trade associations, conventions, and churches. He is also the founder of Try Love Inc., which is a youth leadership development organization that focuses on drug and violence prevention and academic excellence for young people.

Jolley is the author of the international bestseller *It Only Takes a Minute to Change Your Life!*, which has been translated into several languages, and has recorded numerous audio, video, and music albums that capture his unique motivational style. He is a guest columnist with *Black Enterprise* magazine and numerous other publications. Mr. Jolley hosts the syndicated radio show *The Magnificent Motivational Minute* and the national television show *It Only Takes a Minute,* which can be seen on the Success Channel and PBS. Mr. Jolley is the recipient of many awards, including the designation of Certified Speaking Professional from the National Speakers Association. He is a member of the Board of Directors for NSA. He resides in Washington, D.C., with his family.